Best Cliches Ever!
We're Taking Them One at a Time

Dr. Don Powell (a.k.a Dr. Cliche)

Foreword by Mark Cuban

$14.95	8	AA	10
Price	Row	Section	Seat

This book may be taken and reading refused upon refunding the purchase price. If the book is resold or offered for resale at a higher price, it may be seized without any compensation. Reader voluntarily assumes all risks and danger incidental to reading this book, whether it occurred prior to, during, or after reading has taken place, and agrees that the organization, agents, participants, players, the team, and management, are not responsible or liable for any injuries resulting from such cases. This book, if lost or stolen, will not be replaced. Reader may not use alcoholic beverages, bottles, cans, containers, packages, seatbacks, or umbrellas when reading this book. Management reserves the right to eject any person whose conduct it deems disorderly, obnoxious, or unbecoming when reading this book.

No Refunds, Exchanges, or Re-Entry

$14.95	8	AA	10
Price	Row	Section	Seat

Sports Cliches Press

Farmington Hills, Michigan

To my sons Jordan and Brett who make me so proud and who share my passion for sports.

To my wife Nancy for tolerating the tens of thousands of hours I have spent watching sports.

To my mother Yvette and late father Bob for all their love and support.

Copyright © 2004, by Dr. Don Powell (a.k.a. Dr. Cliche)

All Rights Reserved. This copyright book is presented by authority of Sports Cliches, LLC and may not be reproduced or retransmitted in any form, and the accounts and descriptions of this book may not be disseminated, without the express written consent of Sports Cliches, LLC. The views expressed are those of the author and do not necessarily reflect the views of the NFL, NBA, MLB, NHL, PGA, and USTA.

Library of Congress Cataloging-in-Publication Data

Powell, Don R.
    Best Sports Cliches Ever: We're Taking Them One at a Time
    ISBN: 0-9755273-0-4 (trade paperback)
    1. Sports - Cliches. 2. Sports - Expressions. 3. Sports - Sayings. 4. Sports - Language
    Library of Congress Control Number: 2004094256

Cover and book design by Andria Watha
Illustrations by Monica Watha

Published by Sports Cliches Press, Farmington Hills MI
Printed in the United States of America

Best Sports Cliches Ever can be ordered in bulk quantities or in customized editions of any length and look. For more information see the order form on page 192 or contact us at:
Sports Cliches Press
30445 Northwestern Hwy., Ste. 350
Farmington Hills, MI 48334
800.686.7555 or 248.737.6881 • Fax 248.539.1808
email: info@BestSportsCliches.com
www.BestSportsCliches.com

Acknowledgements

Much credit goes to my Sports Cliche Dream Team. Working for the league minimum, these players put their pants on one leg at a time and knew what we needed to succeed. They couldn't have scripted the book any better.

First and foremost, I want to thank my sons Jordan and Brett. They have always stepped up big time for me. Over the years, we have spent endless hours together watching sporting events and noting the cliches. Jordan did a good deal of the book's editing and was my go to guy throughout the project. Brett and I shared many a laugh coming up with the cliche categories. Next I express my appreciation to Sheldon Kay. Over scores of lunches, we ate our words discussing the book. Thanks to buddies Joe Berenholz and Eli Zaret for putting up with my inability to "cheer within myself" during sporting events. My other Dream Teammates are:

Dream Team Line Up Card		
Players	**Position**	**Bats**
1. Paul Sippil	5	R
2. Chuck Kessler	4	R
3. Andy Frank	8	R
4. Carl Frank	9	R
5. Randy Stoughton	6	R
6. John Kushner	7	R
7. Jeremy Gershonowicz	2	R
8. Rick Watnick	3	L
9. Mike Siegel	1	R
Pitchers	**Throws**	
Stu Sakwa	R	
Adam Bottoroff	R	
Andy Sofen	R	
Dominick Osman	R	
Jerry Lewis	R	

Next, I would like to thank my staff at the American Institute for Preventive Medicine who always come to play and ran the company while I worked on this book. Special thanks go to Wendy Fiorentino, my administrative assistant, for typing the manuscript (23 times), Andria Watha for her excellent graphic design work, and Sue Jackson for her marketing and operational skills. Monica Watha did a wonderful job on the illustrations.

Finally, I want to express my appreciation to all the sports announcers, players, and fans who use cliches. They are the book's X-factor and it wouldn't exist if it weren't for them.

Needless to say, the Best Sports Cliches Ever was a total team effort.

About Dr. Don Powell (a.k.a. Dr. Cliche)

Don "Dr. Cliche" Powell is a best selling author, clinical psychologist, corporate CEO, sports afficionado, and lifelong student of the game. He has written 14 books that have sold over 4 million copies and been translated into 5 languages. He also wrote a nationally syndicated newspaper column and articles for Shape magazine. Dr. Powell has won numerous awards for his work, including those from the President's Council on Physical Fitness and Sports, Department of Health and Human Services, U.S. Jaycees, and the State of Michigan.

He has appeared on hundreds of television and radio talk shows, including Good Morning America, CNN, Sonya, Body by Jake, and the CBS, NBC, and ABC radio broadcasting networks. Powell has been written about in many publications, such as USA Today, New York Times, Wall Street Journal, Forbes, and Good Housekeeping. He taught at the University of Michigan and was nominated for the Distinguished Teaching Award. He is presently the President and CEO of the American Institute for Preventive Medicine, a Farmington Hills, MI company that provides health management and wellness programs for thousands of corporations, hospitals, unions, colleges, and the U.S. government.

Other books written by Dr. Don Powell:
- A Year of Health Hints: 365 Practical Ways to Feel Better & Live Longer
- Health at Home®: Your Complete Guide to Symptoms, Solutions, and Self-Care
- Seniors Health at Home®: Guide to Symptoms, Solutions, and Self-Care for Those 50+

A Note from Dr. Cliche

This book is not meant to substitute for actually watching a sporting event on television or in person. Any similarity to cliches used by announcers or players was intentional.

I use the male pronoun "he" throughout the book for simplicity purposes only. The cliches apply equally to female athletes, sportscasters, coaches, and fans. I hope you enjoy reading these cliches as much as I did gathering them.

For more information and activities related to sports cliches, please go to our website. If you know any cliches that are not in this book, I would like hearing them, as well as, your general comments. You can contact me by email or writing to the address below.

Sports Cliche Press
30445 Northwestern Highway, Suite 350
Farmington Hills, MI 48334
248.737.6881 • Fax 248.539.1808

drcliche@BestSportsCliches.com
www.BestSportsCliches.com

Table of Contents

Foreword 14
Words From a Former NBA All Star 15
Introduction 16

Section 1

It's Just One Game
Cliches Across Sports

The Thrill of Victory – Winning Locker Room Cliches 22

The Agony of Defeat – Losing Locker Room Cliches 24

Something Has Got to Give – Game Cliches 26

The Game Is Winding Down – Cliches Just Before the Final Whistle 28

This Is As Big As It Gets – Big Game/Rivalry Cliches 30

There's No "I" in Team – General Team Cliches 32

They Know How to Win – Good Team Cliches 34

This Team Is Beating Itself – Bad Team Cliches 39

He's the Go To Guy – Good Player Cliches 42

He Has His Critics – Poor Player Cliches 46

We Need to Step Up as a Team – Step Cliches 48

He's Come Along Sooner Than Expected – Rookie Cliches 49

He's Had a Storied Career – Veteran Cliches 50

He's a Speed Merchant – Cliches About Speed 52

He's Got Ice Water in His Veins – Cliches Under Pressure 54

When the Going Gets Tough – Toughness Cliches 56

The Game is Bursting With Emotion – Emotion Cliches 57

There Goes the Lady Byng – Fighting Cliches 58

He Had His Bell Rung – Injury Cliches 59

The Clock Is Their Biggest Enemy – Time Cliches 62

He's an X's and O's Man – Coach Cliches 64

The Refs Swallowed Their Whistles – Officiating Cliches 67

The Crowd Is Really Fired Up – Fan Cliches..70

The Trade Was Good for Both Teams – Front Office Cliches 72

It's a Tough Place to Play – Stadium Cliches 74

He's on Fire – Hot Cliches 75

We Look to Our Seniors – College Cliches 76

Section 2

Are You Ready For Some Football?
Football Cliches

It Was a Hard Hitting Game – Game Cliches 80

They're Back on Their Heels – Defense Cliches 82

He Put a Lick On Him – Tackling Cliches 83

They're Moving the Ball at Will – Offense Cliches 84

He Heard Footsteps – Pass Coverage Cliches 86

It's 3 Yards and a Cloud of Dust – Rushing Cliches 87

He Telegraphed That One – Quarterback Cliches 88

He Had Him Beat – Receiving Cliches 90

He Split the Uprights – Kicker Cliches 91

7

Section 3

I Love This Game!

Basketball Cliches

He Got Nothing But Net – Shooting Cliches 94

He Shot It from Downtown – 3 Pointer Cliches 97

He Owns the Glass – Rebounding Cliches..98

He Got His Pocket Picked – Dribbling / Passing Cliches 99

It's Been a Game of Runs – Team Cliches 100

Section 4

Play Ball!

Baseball Cliches

They Have Ducks on the Pond – Game Cliches 104

He Fanned – Strikeout Cliches 105

He Went the Distance – Pitcher Cliches 106

He Ripped the Cover Off the Ball – Batter Cliches 108

He Tattooed That One – Home Run Cliches 110

He Got a Good Jump – Base Running Cliches 112

That Was a Twin Killing – Double Play Cliches 112

He Showed Some Leather – Fielding Cliches 113

Section 5
He Shoots, He Scores
Hockey Cliches

They're Getting Beaten to the Puck – Team Cliches 116
He Stood On His Head – Goalie Cliches 117
He Put the Biscuit In the Basket – Scoring Cliches 118
He Split the Defense – Player Cliches 119

Section 6
He Teed It Up
Golf Cliches

He Won't Be Happy With That Shot – Shot Cliches 122
Here's Making His Charge – Tournament/Course Cliches 124

Section 7
Game, Set, Match
Tennis Cliches

He Bageled Him – Player Cliches 126
He Served Up an Ace – Shot Cliches 127

Section 8

This Game Will Be Won In the Trenches
Sports Cliche Origins

It's a War Out There – Military Cliches 130

We Shot Ourselves in the Foot – Wild West Cliches 132

They Need to Right the Ship – Nautical Cliches 134

He's Pleading His Case – Legal Cliches 135

He Did His Homework – School Cliches 136

He's Paying Dividends – Money Cliches 138

We Got the Monkey Off Our Backs – Animal Cliches 140

They're a Blue Collar Team – Business Cliches 142

They Play In Your Face – Parts of the Body Cliches 143

They Couldn't Have Scripted It Better – Entertainment / Electricity Cliches 146

It's Back to the Drawing Board – Artist Cliches 147

They're Playing for All the Marbles –Hobby Cliches 148

You Can Stick a Fork in Him – Food Cliches 149

He's All Washed Up – Water Cliches 152

He Threw Up a Brick – Construction Cliches 153

He's Nursing an Injury – Medical Cliches 156

It's Do or Die – Life and Death Cliches 158

He Threw Up a Hail Mary – Religious Cliches 160

He's Seeing the Ball Well – Sense Cliches 161

The Drive Stalled – Travel Cliches 164

He Has Some Big Shoes to Fill – Clothing Cliches 167

He Beat All Odds – Gambling/Magic Cliches 169

Section 9
He's In Our Corner
Cliches in the Mainstream

He's On His Game – All Sports 172
He Goes the Extra Yard – Football..173
They Put On a Full Court Press – Basketball 174
He Stepped Up – Baseball 175
They're Running On All Cylinders – Auto Racing...176
He Went Wire to Wire – Horse Racing 177
They Went Toe to Toe – Boxing 178
He Raised the Bar – Track 179

Section 10
Can You Get 110%?
Sports Cliche Quiz

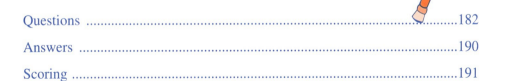

Questions 182
Answers 190
Scoring 191

11

Foreword

Words From a Former NBA All Star

Introduction

Foreword

You have to love this book. As I read through it, two things crossed my mind. First, I could hear some of my favorite all time announcers using the cliches. Second, I would like to hand one of these books to every member of the sports media I have to deal with. I would tell them I won't do any interviews if their questions include any of the cliches from the book. Just the puzzled looks on their faces as they realize they don't have any questions that don't include one of Don's cliches would be priceless.

Best Sports Cliches Ever is a fun read that had me laughing and smiling the entire time. I wholeheartedly recommend it to anyone who enjoys watching, playing, or working in sports. This includes fans, athletes, columnists, talk show hosts, and sportscasters. To members of the media, I beg you to buy this book. Then, please exclude its contents from any future questions you may ask me.

- *Mark Cuban, Owner Dallas Mavericks and Chairman of HDNet*

Words From a Former NBA All Star

During my 11 seasons as an NBA player, I spent countless hours in the locker room and on the court. During these times, I heard teammates, opponents, coaches, sportscasters, and fans use thousands of cliches. As a stutterer, I also used cliches because they say so much in so few words. Cliches were also helpful growing up with 13 brothers and sisters. It was tough to get a word in edgewise and cliches allowed me to say things quickly and simply.

One of my favorite cliches was "kill a gnat with a sledgehammer". This means that you should never take it easy on a weaker team. That's because you never know when the momentum might change and you could end up losing in an upset. "You've got to step up big time" is a cliche I learned from my high school coach. I even use cliches like "he turned a negative into a positive" in my motivational speeches.

I always thought it would be great if someone gathered all the different sports cliches and put them in a book. Then I met Dr. Don Powell, the author of Best Sports Cliches Ever. Don is a funny guy and he has done an incredible job of not only gathering cliches, but dividing them into humorous categories. Just about everything in the book contains cliches, including the acknowledgments, introduction, table of contents, and, of course, the chapters. There's even a quiz to test your cliche knowledge. Don Powell is truly the Doctor of Cliches.

This book is funny, clever, entertaining, and interesting. It's "got the whole package" and makes great reading for both children and adults. It's "a slam dunk" to make all the best seller lists and Dr. Cliche is "a real gamer" who has "Hall of Fame written all over him". The book should be on the bookshelf or coffee table of any man or woman who considers themselves a true sports fan.

- Bob "Butterbean" Love; 3 Time NBA All Star; Director of Community Relations, Chicago Bulls

Introduction

As a *student of the game*, I always wondered whether it was better to *step up big time* or *take it up a notch; play within yourself* or *come to play*; have *a world of speed* or be *a speed merchant; ooze confidence* or *measure your words carefully*. The various cliches and expressions used in sports have always held a fascination for me as they do for 88 million fellow sports fans. This may be due to the fact that fans spend countless hours each year watching their favorite pastimes.

Webster's Dictionary defines a cliche as "a trite phrase or expression; something that has become overly familiar or commonplace". Cliches express a lot in just a few words and thus are quoted over and over and over and over. In the fast changing and uncertain times we live in today, there is something soothing about things that are common and familiar. They provide comfort and trust; they make us feel good. This is why so many people enjoy antiques, classic cars, songs from their teens, and aging rock groups. Good feelings can also be produced by words, including cliches, as they make an emotional connection with us.

We have a love-hate relationship with cliches. Although we complain about them, we are also enamored with them. We criticize athletes and announcers when they use them, yet we use them ourselves. That's because they always seem to fit.

Cliches allow us to communicate in a more simplified manner using a unique, colorful language. This brings people together. Using cliches allows us to join a "fan" club. We demonstrate our expertise about a particular sport and communicate with other club members. This "members only" club excludes people who don't know the lingo. It's like having a secret handshake. We may even view people who don't understand a cliche as rookies with little knowledge of the game.

Cliches also allow us to say the same thing in many different ways. For example, when someone is tackled in football, *he was hammered, stuffed, stuck, clotheslined, popped, unloaded on, punished,* or *wrapped up*. When a player scores in basketball, *he buried, filled, sticked, nailed, dropped, swished, drained,* or *hit it*.

Coaches and athletes are notorious for using cliches. In an article that appeared in the Detroit Free Press here's what Detroit Pistons' coach Larry Brown had to say after a game. Depending upon your definition, there are 6 - 8 cliches in the paragraph below.

> "I sensed at half-time that *they had a lot of energy*. I thought in the first half *we tried to trade baskets* with them. *We got some stops.* Once we got a lead, *we executed a lot better*. I thought *the defense was really the key down the stretch.* Rip (Hamilton) had a *very tough match up*. The fact that he guarded well *down the stretch* and also had the energy to score *was big*."

Then you have Rip's assessment of his own performance. He tops his coach with 9 cliches.

> "I think the guys did *a great job of finding me* and giving me *opportunities to get open*. I just tried *to keep moving*, *play my game*, but also stay patient, *stay in the flow of the offense* and *try to make shots. I have been feeling it* for awhile. I'm trying *to learn the system. I'm just being patient* and having fun."

Cliches are so disdained that many interviewees will apologize for using them. How many times have you heard someone say, "I hate to use a cliche," and then go on to use a cliche. We also hear people justify the use of a cliche by identifying one before saying it. For example, prior to the 2004 Rose Bowl against USC, University of Michigan football coach Lloyd Carr said,

> "It's become a cliche to *talk about the trenches*, but this game, *more than any I can remember*, will be *won or lost right there*."

Actually Coach Carr included 2 additional cliches in his statement.

Many cliches apply only to sports – *they have ducks on the pond* or *he went top shelf*. Some have been taken from other areas of life and are now used in sports – *they put the nail in the coffin* or *they are a Cinderella story*. Then there are sports cliches that originated within a sport and have become part of everyday language – *he raised the bar* or the *ball's in your court*. We have military cliches – *this game will be won in the trenches*, nautical cliches – *they need to batten down the hatches*, wild west cliches – *the wheels are falling off the wagon*, education cliches – *he schooled him*, financial cliches – *he's paying dividends*, fighting cliches – *they're mucking it up in the corner*, religious cliches – *he committed a cardinal sin*, business cliches – *they're a blue collar team* and the list goes on.

17

Cliches are everywhere. They are a part of the fabric of life. They are woven into not only sporting events, but everyday conversation. Many of the cliches in this book came from my conversations with others. From now on, pay attention to what you and others say and I'm certain that *110% of the time*, a cliche is used.

Quite frankly, in some ways, we can't live without sports cliches. They have become as much a part of sports as the games themselves. This explains why many sportscasters have become as well known as the players and coaches.

I stopped gathering sports cliches after I reached 3,289. I then assembled and coached a group of *sports cliche aficionados*. I wasn't interested in the best individual aficionado, but rather those who *would play well together*, as *there's no "I" in team*. This *dream team* then rated each cliche as to its clicheness. The team *was a force to be reckoned with* and *knew how to win*. Unfortunately, there were a lot of *egos in the locker room* and *harmony didn't always exist. Faced with a renewed sense of urgency*, however, *we brought our A game* and selected the best cliches.

Each section in the book begins with a short vignette. cliches are then listed. Those with an underlined word indicate ones where any number of words can be inserted to complete the cliche, i.e., *We need to win the <u>turnover battle</u>*. Cliches
(Fill in factor)
with a slash (/) and without the underline contain two interchangeable words either of which can form a cliche, i.e., *He's trying to hit/shoot his way out of a slump*.

You'll also notice that on the side of each right hand page there is a ticket. The section number stands for the chapter and the seat is the page number.

In organizing the sections, I found it interesting to see which cliches applied to which sport. Many cliches are used in more than one sport. They appear in Section 1, titled **It's Just One Game**. Examples include *they had a scare today, it doesn't get any better than this, we found a way to win*, or *we came up big time*. Of the major sports, football and basketball have the most cliches that overlap; for example, *he couldn't find the handle, he schooled him, the play/shot clock is winding down,* and *he was stripped of the ball* apply to both sports.

Section 2, titled **Are You Ready for Some Football!** addresses cliches that are used exclusively in football. Football is the sport that not only has the most cliches, but also the most categories – nine. In fact, there are as many cliches for quarterbacks as there are in all of tennis.

Section 3, **I Love This Game!** presents cliches unique to basketball, Section 4, **Play Ball!** lists baseball cliches while Section 5, **He Shoots, He Scores** is devoted to hockey. Section 6, **He Teed It Up** addresses golf and Section 7, **Game, Set, Match** covers tennis which is the sport with the fewest cliches.

Section 8, **This Game Will Be Won in the Trenches** presents the origins of many sports cliches. It is fascinating to see how many cliches originate from the fields of education, business, finance, travel, construction, law, etc. There are 24 categories in this chapter, but others could have been added. After each cliche, I designate which section it would normally be listed in.

Section 9, **He's In Our Corner**, presents expressions that started in one sport, but are now used as cliches in other sports or have become cliches in everyday language. Examples include *they need to pick up the pace*, *the ball's in your court*, *he's in a slump*, *he's up against the ropes*, or *he hit a home run*.

Section 10, **Can You Get 110%?**, provides readers with an opportunity to test their own knowledge of cliches. You can find out if you're a "Cliche King", "X-Factor", "Student of the Game", "Bench Warmer", or "Choke Artist".

This book is my effort to share the sports cliche arena with you. I want to show you the secret handshake and initiate you into the club. Whether you are an avid sports fan, a casual one, or simply a *boo bird*, these cliches will either *have you buzzing in your seats* or *sitting on your hands*. The one thing they will not do is *come back to haunt you*.

Section 1

It's Just One Game

Clichés Across Sports

The Thrill of Victory
Winning Locker Room Clichés

> It was a *great come from behind victory* for the Padres today although it *was an ugly one*. Despite winning 8 - 5, *the score was not indicative* of how close the game really was. The heavily favored Twins *played uninspired baseball*. *Jubilation was the word of the day* in the Padre locker room. Jordan Scott, their star shortstop crowed *"We got the big one today. I know it wasn't pretty,* but *a win is a win. Everyone has been counting us out,* but *we believed in ourselves."*

We came up big time.

We needed this one.

That was an ugly win.

It was a total team effort.

It doesn't get any better than this.

We're **happy** to **win** any way we can.

It was the kind of game that can turn their season around.

They played inspired <u>baseball</u>.
(fill in sport)

We had every excuse to just lay down, but we didn't.

It's still a "W".

They find new ways to win.

The score was not indicative of how close the game really was.

They sent a message today.

That's why they play both halves/the game.

We played our game.

22

We took them out of their game.

The bigger they are, the harder they fall.

All that matters is that we got the win.

They got back in the win column.

We just kept fighting.

We knew what we needed to do to win.

We don't have time to celebrate.

We hung in there.

They played well down the stretch.

We're just happy with the win.

It doesn't matter how we win.

Everyone had been counting us out.

We put ourselves in a position to win.

They had a scare today.

We wanted it more.

This game was a defining moment for us.

They made the plays when they needed to.

This has got to be our biggest win.

1	AA	23
Sec	Row	Seat

The Agony of Defeat

Losing Locker Room Clichés

> It was *a somber Kings' locker room* after Saturday's game. It was clear the *players took the loss very hard.* Brett Ryan was one of the first players to speak up telling anyone who would listen that *"we were beaten soundly* and *lost to a better team.* "But", he added wistfully, "on the other hand, *we failed to capitalize on our opportunities. I've never been this frustrated,* but *it's time to move on."*

There's always tomorrow.

Nobody in the locker room feels worse than he does.

We played uninspired <u>hockey</u>.
(fill in sport)

We need to put this one behind us.

We came up/fell short.

We **embarrassed** ourselves out there.

We didn't play like we're capable of.

We lost to a good <u>basketball</u> team.
(fill in sport)

I hate to say it, but it looks like they gave up.

We played well enough to win.

We need to get back to our winning ways.

Losing is never easy.

Records mean nothing if you don't win.

The better team won.

It's time to move on.

They pretty much had their way with us.

They took us out of our game plan.

We didn't get it done.

We don't have any excuses.

They made the plays and we didn't.

It's just **one game.**

They wanted it more than we did.

We all but handed them the game.

It's a long season.

The coach can't make plays – only we can.

We beat ourselves.

We just have to prepare better next game.

Their worst fears came true.

Our dreams were shattered.

They took it to us.

It just wasn't our day.

We only have ourselves to blame.

We beat them in all aspects of the game except the score.

1	AA	25
Sec	Row	Seat

Something Has Got to Give

Game Clichés

We've got *an exciting game on our hands today* between the Pacers and the Pistons. *It has playoff implications and you can feel the tension down on the floor.* Both teams *appear to be sizing up one another* in the early going. *This is always a tough arena* for the opposition to play in. It will all, however, *come down to execution* and *who makes their free throws* when *they count most.*

How do you account for what's happening out there?

The difference in the game was <u>their defense</u>.
                                             (fill in factor)

This game has play-off implications.

Expansion has diluted the league's talent/hurt the quality of play.

I think the <u>Sharks</u> are going to be in for a surprise.
        (fill in team)

You make your own breaks.

You can **feel** the **momentum** changing.

They need to play well for all 60 minutes.

Statistics don't lie.

The pundits say <u>he'll have a great game</u>.
                        (fill in anything)

They have to be wondering what hit them.

They don't look like they have a clue.

Both teams are on edge.

They're making a game of it.

They need to make some adjustments at half-time.

It's good for the game of <u>baseball</u>.
(fill in sport)

This game is wide open.

They need to get something going here.

They're locked up in a tight one.

This will **separate** the **men** from the **boys.**

You can't teach the intangibles.

The <u>crowd</u> is the X-factor in this game.
(fill in factor)

No one expected this.

The outcome will be decided by <u>free throws</u>.
(fill in factor)

Just when I thought I saw everything.

It's a game of inches.

It's not how you start, it's how you finish.

It's not a sprint, it's a marathon.

If they are going to win, they have to <u>play smarter</u>.
(fill in factor)

They are having their way with them.

They came up big.

They are controlling the tempo of the game.

They're playing with them.

It's only a matter of time before they score.

They are being outplayed in all facets of the game.

1	AA	27
Sec	Row	Seat

The Game Is Winding Down

Clichés Just Before the Final Whistle

> *Who could have predicted this?* The Panthers have *been a Cinderella story all season,* but *it looks like their luck's run out.* This is an *extremely important possession for them.* If they don't capitalize here, *it's lights out.* I'm not sure, but *it might be time to push the panic button.* There's *no room for error.*

Now they have some breathing room.

This game has become a laugher.

It ain't over til it's over.

This game's up for grabs.

This game is getting out of control/hand.

That sealed the victory.

The game comes down to this play.

They're really starting to put it to them.

They're starting to put them away.

It's too little, too late.

This is an important possession.

This game has overtime written all over it.

The party's over.

The game is on the line.

It's anyone's game.

They are not out of the woods yet.

The game is going down to the wire.

You can turn out the lights.

Start the bus, the party's over.

They need a stop here.

They are letting them hang around.

It's been all <u>Cowboys</u> today.
(fill in team)

Their final attempt at a rally was thwarted.

All of a sudden, we've got a game.

This game has really turned around.

There's **no** room for **error**.

They're playing not to lose.

Their chances are slim and none and slim just left the building.

1	AA	29
Sec	Row	Seat

This Is As Big As It Gets
Big Game/Rivalry Clichés

There's no love lost between the Rangers and the Devils. I know *each team circled this game on their schedules* before the season began. *It's a huge game for both franchises,* but the Rangers are *in a must win situation. This game makes or breaks their season. They need to win at all costs.* A loss here and *they'll be playing for pride alone.*

There's no lost love between these two teams.

This **rivalry** is always **great fun**.

We circled this game on our calendar.

This game is our season.

Their playoff hope/season is on the line.

These two teams just plain don't like each other.

This **game** is what you **dream** about as a kid.

This game can make or break their season.

They're the best team we will have played so far.

They face a stiff test today.

We noted <u>Green Bay</u> on the schedule right at the start of the season.
       (fill in opponent)

It's a great match-up.

It's a clash of titans.

There's no tomorrow.

This is a huge game for us.

These teams match up well.

They are in a must win situation.

It's a David vs. Goliath story.

They are two evenly matched teams.

Both teams know each other so well.

This game is a grudge match.

We need to play them one at a time.

You can throw out the record book when these two teams meet.

1	AA	31
Sec	Row	Seat

There's No "I" in Team
General Team Clichés

The Avalanche and the Red Wings are *headed in opposite directions this season. The jury is still out* on the Colorado goal tending and *they face a daunting challenge* this evening. For the Red Wings on the other hand, *there are similarities between this year's team and last year's* playoff finalist. *They are strong up front and their goal tending is sound.* In fact, in the last 11 games, they have posted an 8 - 2 - 1 record. Goalie Steve Carabol *has never played better between the pipes* and *is at the top of his game.*

We're all in this together.

The team that wants it more will prevail.

Both teams are in need of a win today.

Ultimately, it comes down to what happens on the field.

It looks like there's some mis-communication out there.

They have a daunting challenge.

They play good fundamental <u>football</u>.
(fill in sport)

It's tough to continue to play at this high a level.

They are happy to go into the locker room with a <u>3</u> point lead.
(fill in #)

They need to come mentally prepared.

They made some adjustments at half-time.

We still **want to be playing** in <u>October</u>.
(fill in month)

They can compete with anyone.

We need to get everybody involved.

Offense wins games, defense wins championships.

We need to go out and just do our job.

We know what's at stake.

We need to pull together as a team.

They're playing a bunch of also rans.

They have to **turn** up the **intensity**.

They need to be thinking out of the box.

They pulled out all the stops.

They're coming off a big win/heartbreaking loss.

You gotta dance with the one who brought ya.

They're just happy to be there.

The only score we need to worry about is our own.

We just need to play our game.

They're on the bubble.

We have to play within ourselves.

They Know How to Win

Good Team Clichés

> The Cowboys *are no fluke this year. They are not an easy team to defend* and *always keep themselves in the game. They are fundamentally sound on both sides of the ball* and *are playing as well as anybody in the league.* In addition, *they are a cohesive unit, both on and off the field.* As their coach, Frank Beal, has said, "There's a lot of love in that locker room."

To be the best, you have to beat the best.

On paper, <u>they are a great team</u>.
(fill in anything)
If we play like we're capable, no one can beat us.

They play well as a team.

Every player understands his role.

The pendulum has swung in their favor.

There is no quit in this team.

They have a good nucleus in place.

They're not willing to rest on their laurels.

They have certainly turned things around.

Right now, they can play with anyone.

They shut down their <u>passing</u> game.
(fill in skill)

They've been a Cinderella story all season.

They are starting to play as a team.

They are a force to be reckoned with.

They're making the most of their opportunities.

They are keeping their opponents off balance.

There's a lot of mystique surrounding this team.

They make the plays when they need to.

This team is no fluke.

They have a definite edge in <u>relief pitching</u>.
(fill in skill)

They have gotten the most out of their talent.

This team has the talent to go all the way.

They just don't give up.

They are not an easy team to defend.

They are going to be tough to beat.

The way they've been playing, they're going to be hard to beat.

1	AA	35
Sec	Row	Seat

They are going to let it all hang out today.

We know what to expect.

They come out and make plays.

They're bringing it.

There's no quit in this team.

They've had to overcome a lot of adversity.

They are a good come from behind team.

They have good ball/puck movement.

They are playing with confidence.

They are going to surprise some people.

They picked it up.

They play a <u>tough</u> brand of <u>football</u>.
          (fill in factor)   (fill in sport)

They are a team without weaknesses.

If they have a weakness, I would like to know what it is.

You can't have enough/too much <u>pitching</u>.
(fill in skill)

This is where we want to be.

They are a team with a mission.

They have **good team chemistry**.

They are a difficult team to stop.

There's a lot of love in that locker room.

They don't want to peak too soon.

They can give you some trouble.

If things weren't bad enough, they just got worse.

This team has a renewed sense of urgency.

They came on like gang busters.

They're the team to beat.

> They play with a lot of swagger.

There are a lot of egos in that locker room.

They're finally learning to play with one another.

We've been there before.

This team is starting to gel.

They **left it all** out on the field.

Right now, they are playing as good as anybody in the country.

They came to play.

They control their own destiny/fate.

They can be a **dangerous team**.

They get the most out of their talent.

They play as a cohesive unit.

They're playing to the level of the competition.

They're right in the thick of things.

This Team Is Beating Itself
Bad Team Clichés

> The Cubs *always seem to get off to a slow start* and this spring is no different. "We were outhit and out-coached today," said Red Battis, their skipper. *"Our poor play has finally caught up with us.* We just *haven't been playing up to our potential.* Squandering a 4 run lead in the 8th inning was clearly our undoing. *We need to develop more of a killer instinct.* Otherwise in September, *we'll just be playing out the string."*

They need to turn things around.

We need to get over the hump.

We've been out <u>played/skated/hustled</u>.
(fill in skill)

They never got it going today.

We haven't been **playing up** to our potential.

They are playing out the string.

They are playing for next season.

They're playing for pride.

They're playing the role of spoiler.

They were taken to the woodshed.

There isn't a **quick fix.**

This team lacks <u>direction/desire/focus</u>.
(fill in attitude)

The team is dealing with a lot of distractions.

They're one of the most penalized teams in the league.

1   AA   39
Sec   Row   Seat

They called a players only meeting.

They have been in a __6__ game skid.
                    (fill in #)

I can't remember the last time we <u>dropped so many passes</u>.
                                        (fill in mistake)

They sealed their own fate.

They always seem to get off to a slow start.

They seem a little rusty after the layoff.

The opposition compounded their woes.

They botched the <u>double play</u>.
                  (fill in skill)

They've had trouble with <u>penalties</u>.
                          (fill in factor)

They need to play better if they want to go anywhere this season.

They made it more difficult on themselves than they had to.

They have been playing better than their record indicates.

The poor play has finally caught up with them.

There's no excuse for so many <u>penalties</u>.
                                (fill in mistake)

We will find out what we are made of soon enough.

You try not to be in that situation.

They're playing out of sync.

They won't get any sympathy from the <u>Knicks</u>.
(fill in team)

They look tentative out there.

They don't have any answers for <u>Michael Jordan</u>.
(fill in player)

They're a one dimensional team.

The offense has bogged down.

Their comeback fell short.

They could be in for a long day.

They've had an up and down season.

They **gift wrapped** this one.

They'll need to regroup in the second half.

They have nothing to lose.

We have to find a way to win.

They're getting raked over the coals.

They're getting the short end of the stick.

They're making things difficult for themselves.

They find new ways to lose.

It looks like there's a little confusion out there.

1	AA	41
Sec	Row	Seat

He's the Go To Guy
Good Player Clichés

The one thing you can say about Ronald James is that *he eats, drinks, and sleeps basketball. He worked hard during the off season to get where he is today. He's the cornerstone of this team* and clearly *they're building the offense around him. He's a complete player* and *commands attention from the opposing team. They have to know where he is at all times. He's made a career out of improvising* off the dribble.

He oozes confidence.

He puts the team before himself.

He represents everything that is good about the game.

He makes things happen.

No one can guard him one on one.

He has a scorer's mentality.

He's finally getting his due.

He works as hard as anybody in this league.

He's had success at all levels.

He's got the whole package.

He's been nothing short of spectacular.

He's the greatest name in <u>auto racing</u>.
                               (fill in sport)

He's put up some very impressive numbers.

· This game will be a defining moment for _____.
                                              (fill in player)

Row
Seat
Price

Section 1

He kept his composure.

He eats, drinks, and sleeps <u>tennis</u>.
(fill in sport)

He's conducts himself well both on and off the field.

He comes highly touted.

He always shows up.

We need to get him more involved.

He adds/gives you another dimension.

He has made a career out of <u>timely hits</u>.
(fill in skill)

They need to give him the ball more.

He showed me a lot today.

He all but guaranteed a victory.

I couldn't ask for anything more from _____.
(fill in player)

He's provided an offensive/defensive spark.

He has what it takes.

He gives opposing teams fits.

He'd rather let his actions on the field speak for himself.

1	AA	43
Sec	Row	Seat

There aren't too many people in the league who can do what he does.

He answered the call.

That will make the highlight reel.

He's a real presence out there.

He was poised down the stretch.

He sees the whole <u>field/court/floor/ice</u>.
(fill in surface)

He can hurt you in so many ways.

He turned a negative into a positive.

He has the uncanny ability to <u>block shots</u>.
(fill in skill)

He capped off a great season.

He's really coming into his own.

He's done all we could ask.

I can't say enough about _____.
(fill in player)

He's taking over the game.

He relies upon his athleticism.

He gives 110%.

He does all the little things.

He's all about winning.

He's something special.

He's a playmaker.

He's an impact player.

He's a prime/big time player.

He has good instincts.

He's a real gamer.

He's a coach's dream.

He's the main man.

He can turn it on and off.

He's a streaky <u>shooter</u>.
(fill in skill)

You can't stop him, you only hope to contain him.

1	AA	45
Sec	Row	Seat

He Has His Critics

Poor Player Clichés

The fortunes of the Canadians *clearly rest with their star forward,* Joe Berens. Unfortunately, Berens was *trying to do too much today* and *never was able to get into a rhythm. His ill-advised penalty* near the end of the second period was costly. Berens acknowledged that *he's been struggling a bit lately.* His coach, Maurice Jackson, however, defended him by saying that in critical situations, I want Joe on the ice. *This team will sink or swim* with Joe Berens.

He wasn't able to get into a rhythm.

It looks like he's just going through the motions.

He's been **struggling** a bit **lately**.

He's trying to do too much.

He needs to take better care of the ball.

He went public with his frustration.

He's a derisive force in the clubhouse.

He's his own worst enemy/critic.

He's trying to hit/shoot his way out of a slump.

He couldn't hit the broadside of a barn.

He has been complaining about his playing/ice time all season.

He displayed a lackluster performance.

He's been known to toot this own horn.

He makes no apologies.

The one rap on his game is that he <u>shoots too much</u>.
(fill in weakness)

He's been through a lot.

He's bounced around the league.

I don't want to become a distraction to my team.

He's been reading too many of his press clippings.

My words were taken out of context.

He's no stranger to controversy.

I apologize if I offended anyone.

He's not had any kind of season to speak of.

We Need to Step Up as a Team

Step Clichés

He stepped right in. – *Good Player*

He stepped up big time. – *Good Player*

He stepped up into the pocket. – *Quarterback*

They have really stepped it up. – *Team*

Someone needs to step up. – *Team*

We have to step up to the next level. – *Team*

He's Come Along Sooner Than Expected

Rookie Clichés

LeBron Edwards is *taking advantage of his opportunities*. Even though *he's the new kid on the block*, he demonstrates *a maturity beyond his years*. Even his veteran teammate, Lonny "Sky" Walker, thinks *"He has a great future in this league. He's eager to learn"*.

Positive Clichés

He has a maturity beyond his years.

He's the new kid on the block.

They think he'll be a great one.

He's a can't miss prospect.

He has a great future in this league.

He's taking advantage of his opportunities.

He has superstar written all over him.

He wants to show that he belongs in this league.

Negative Clichés

He still has to learn the ropes.

They went right at him.

He needs more game experience.

He's green behind the ears.

He still has a lot to learn.

He made a rookie mistake.

1	AA	49
Sec	Row	Seat

He's Had a Storied Career
Veteran Clichés

John Montoya has had *a long and illustrious career in the league.* His trade to the Blues has given him *a new lease on life.* Now that he's older, *he's clearly playing smarter.* There was talk that he was *all washed up* and *past his prime,* but when you talk to him, you can see that *the fire burns* and *the intensity is still there.*

Positive Clichés

He's been in this league for a long time.

Now that he's older, he's playing smarter.

He's been with them for many campaigns.

He's a wily veteran.

He's a seasoned veteran.

He's had a stellar career.

He's been around the block.

The intensity is still there.

That's the exclamation point on a sterling career.

He's a legend of the gridiron.

He's had a Hall of Fame career.

He still has a lot of <u>tennis</u> left in him.
(fill in sport)

He's meant so much to this franchise.

He's on his way to <u>Cooperstown</u>.
(fill in Hall of Fame)

He's a veteran <u>hurler</u>.
(fill in position)

He's a sentimental favorite.

Put him down with the great ones.

He's a <u>baseball</u> legend.
(fill in sport)

He brings a lot of experience to the team / position.

Negative Clichés

He's past his prime.

He's seen better days.

He's in the twilight of his career.

He's lost a step.

His body has taken a beating over the years.

He's a journeyman <u>second baseman</u>.
(fill in position)

All the games have taken a toll on his body.

> He still has a love for the game.

He's a Speed Merchant

Clichés About Speed

Speed is something *you just can't teach*. Deion Staller *has quick feet, accelerates well,* and *can cut on a dime.* He *has breakneck speed* and *once he gets ahead of the field, it's off to the races. No one can catch him.*

He accelerates well.

He has quick feet.

He has deceptive speed.

He uses his speed and quickness.

He's a speed demon.

He's a thoroughbred.

He has breakaway speed.

He put on the afterburners.

He showed a good burst of speed.

He had a full head of steam.

He's ahead of the field.

No one will catch him.

He has good wheels.

He can cut on a dime.

He turned on the jets.

He's fleet footed.

He can fly.

He has a world of speed.

1	AA	53
Sec	Row	Seat

He's Got Ice Water in His Veins
Clichés Under Pressure

Frank Adcock *is a pressure player.* There are other players who *get rattled in these situations,* but not Adcock. *He thrives on pressure. When the game's on the line, he's as cool as the other side of the pillow.* He always seems *to come through in the clutch.*

Positive Clichés

He thrives under pressure.

They brought pressure.

He doesn't get rattled out there.

He doesn't fold under pressure.

He came through in the clutch.

He's a pressure player.

He's as cool as the other side of the pillow.

Negative Clichés

He's a choke artist.

He's been known to crack under pressure.

He couldn't handle the pressure.

They put pressure on him.

He seems rattled.

It was a pressure packed game.

They came with inside/outside pressure.

This game is a real pressure cooker.

The players are starting to feel the pressure.

1	AA	55
Sec	Row	Seat

When the Going Gets Tough

Toughness Clichés

That was a tough catch.

He picked up some tough yards.

He sank a tough putt.

He has a tough lie.

He nailed a tough shot.

He throws a tough sinker.

That was a tough play.

That was a tough pick-up.

That was a tough in-between hop.

He needs to tough it out.

He's hanging tough.

That was a tough call.

This was a tough loss/win.

This team has tremendous mental toughness.

The Game is Bursting With Emotion

Emotion Clichés

They're playing with alot of emotion.

They had an emotional letdown.

He doesn't let his feelings bubble over.

He's feeling it.

He's pumped.

The game is already bursting with emotion.

They need to keep their emotions in check.

1	AA	57
Sec	Row	Seat

There Goes the Lady Byng
Fighting Clichés

There was extracurricular activity after the play.

A fracas has broken out.

They had a brouhaha.

There's a donnybrook going on down there.

There's a rhubarb out on the field.

They're mucking it up in the corner.

They dropped their gloves.

He gave him a facial.

They're going at it in the corner.

They're exchanging pleasantries.

They got into it.

They squared off.

Tempers flared, but cooler heads prevailed.

There's a lot of jawing going on.

They aired their differences at a team meeting.

They are at odds with one another.

He can trash talk with the best of them.

He Had His Bell Rung
Injury Clichés

Injuries are part of the game, but the Heat have had *more than their share.* In the last game alone, Ricky Corts twisted his ankle and *has been walking very gingerly* ever since. *He's clearly not 100%* and *will be in street clothes today. He's listed as day-to-day.*

Positive for a Player

He could have played today if they needed him.

He got the wind knocked out of him.

It looks like it's just a stinger.

He fights through his injuries.

You know if there's any way he could play, he would.

He's trying to work his way back into the line-up.

He's good to go.

He plays through his injuries.

He's walking off under his own steam.

That was a scary moment down there.

Everyone can breathe a collective sigh of relief.

He plays through the pain.

He plays hurt.

He's a quick healer.

Negative for a Player

He didn't suit up for today's game.

He tested it during warmups, but still couldn't go.

He's had a season ending injury.

He doesn't want to come back too soon.

He's walking gingerly.

They are saving him for next week.

He looks a little gimpy.

I won't play if it will hurt the team.

You know it has to be tough watching from the sidelines.

He's listed as day-to-day.

His status remains unknown.

He's going to sit this one out.

He's not expected to start/play.

He went down with an injury.

You hate to see an injury like this.

You don't wish an injury like that on anyone.

It hurts to watch that from up here.

He's not 100%.

He's very injury prone.

Injuries to a Team

They're all banged up.

They need to stay healthy.

They have been decimated by injuries.

Injuries have played a big role.

Injuries have taken their toll.

Injuries are part of the game.

We're really beat up.

They are injury ridden.

We're a bit nicked up.

> We have a lot of bumps and bruises.

The Clock Is Their Biggest Enemy

Time Clichés

They're into *their 2 minute offense* and *have their full complement of time outs remaining.* There's *still a lot of time left,* but *they'll have to hurry* as they need 2 scores. Unfortunately, *there's some confusion at the line of scrimmage* so they'll have *to burn their first time out.*

They've got to hurry to get the play off.

They managed the clock well.

That play used up a lot of clock.

They didn't use their timeouts wisely.

They're into their two minute drill.

He just got the shot off.

Fifteen seconds seem like an eternity.

The clock is their ally.

There is still a lot of <u>football</u> to play.
(fill in sport)
There's still a lot of time left.

Now is the time to run some clock.

They need to use more clock.

They used good clock management.

They made good use of the clock.

They are in their hurry up offense.

The play/shot clock is winding down.

They still have their full complement of timeouts.

You don't want to take the timeouts into the locker room with you.

1	AA	63
Sec	Row	Seat

He's an X's and O's Man
Coach Clichés

Bill Brown's teams *are notorious slow starters* and this season has been no different. Some of his players have privately wished he would *open up the play book* despite the fact he has been known as *a defensive wizard* throughout his career. Brown has been unhappy with his team's play thus far, but said he is *not planning to make any major changes* at this point in the season. *"We just have to maintain our focus."* Clearly *the players have been behind him,* but *an extended losing streak could change all that.*

He's a defensive/offensive minded coach.

We need to keep our focus.

He's a game day coach.

They are a well coached team.

We need to shake off last week's disappointment.

_____ and _____ have locked horns all season.
(fill in coach)   (fill in player)

He pulled all the right strings.

He went in with a good game plan.

He has the respect of his players.

I'm thankful for the opportunity to coach a great group of kids/men/ladies.

They want to talk it over.

We may tinker with our offense a little.

They did all I could have asked of them.

I question the play calling.

I'll have to see who really wants to play.

It will be a game time decision.

This team reflects the personality of their coach.

I came here to do a job.

He's lost the team.

You have to be happy for _____.
(fill in coach)

His teams are notorious slow starters.

He needs to open up the play book.

He's been there before.

We've decided to go in a different direction.

He has a groundswell of support.

They've given him a vote of confidence.

He makes good adjustments at half time.

The players have bought into his system.

If I knew it would turn out the way it did, I wouldn't have done it.

The front office is behind him.

I don't know what he said at half time, but it worked.

I'm more proud of this team than any other.

There will be a lot of second guessing about that call.

We need to break down the film.

I don't know where we go from here.

He's clearly not happy with his team's play.

The Refs Swallowed Their Whistles
Officiating Clichés

This has been *an error filled game* and the *penalty flags have been flying.* I think the Vikings *have every right to be upset* as *the refs have not been calling it both ways.* Right now, the officials *are huddling up to discuss the penalty. The request for review is coming from upstairs.* Once again, there must *be definitive, indisputable visual evidence to overturn the decision on the field.* Sure enough, the official *is waving off the flag.*

The officials are reviewing the play.

The request for review is coming from upstairs.

The official is waving off the flag.

He jumped/got in there early.

He lined up in the neutral zone.

They gave him a good spot.

All you want is for the refs to be consistent.

They have every right to be upset.

That was a needless penalty.

1	AA	67
Sec	Row	Seat

There must be definitive, indisputable visual evidence to overturn the decision on the field.

The initial ruling down on the field is <u>holding</u>.
(fill in penalty)

This is an error-filled game.

Someone forgot the snap count.

This one is coming back.

He knows what he can get away with and what he can't.

He got a piece of him.

No harm, No foul.

He got away with one.

The refs are calling everything.

The refs are calling it both ways.

He got tossed.

He got T'd up.

And one!

That was a ticky tack foul.

That was a homer call.

He picks up fouls in bunches.

The officials are letting the game get out of control.

The ref had no choice but to call that one.

The referees are letting them play.

There's a lot of linen on the field.

That was a good no call.

That was a good piece of officiating.

1	AA	69
Sec	Row	Seat

The Crowd Is Really Fired Up
Fan Clichés

Today we have *a sell-out crowd* and *the fans are loving it*. The Yankees have some of *the most vocal fans in the league* and *they are getting their money's worth*. Some of *the Yankee faithful* have even *brought out their brooms*.

Happy Fans

The crowd's giving them a standing O.

It's a sell-out crowd.

There's standing room only.

The <u>Kings</u> faithful are getting what they came for.
(fill in team)

The fans are going crazy.

They're bringing noise.

The crowd goes wild.

They have some of the most vocal fans in the league.

The crowd is in a frenzy.

The fans have brought out the brooms.

The crowd is their 6th/12th man.

The fans are really into it.

70

He's a sports afficionado.

The fans are still buzzing over that one.

He's a real crowd pleaser.

The fans are loving it.

He ignited the crowd.

The fans are making communication difficult.

Unhappy Fans

The fans want to see something happen.

He's an Monday morning quarterback.

That play silenced the crowd.

The **crowd** is growing **restless.**

The crowd wanted a whistle.

He took the crowd out of the game.

The fans are sitting on their hands.

The crowd is letting the home team hear it.

The Trade Was Good for Both Teams
Front Office Clichés

> They've been trying to trade Jeff Teague since the All Star break. In fact, he's been playing a lot more of late as *they want to showcase him*. Unfortunately, only *a handful of teams in the league can take on his contract*. His no-trade clause also *limits his marketability*. Even if a trade does not take place, *they will surely part ways at* the end of the season.

Trades

He has a no trade clause in his contract.

They made some good trades in the off season.

They got him off the waiver wire.

He's excited about being here.

You won't recognize this team next year.

There will be a lot of changes during the off season.

They'll listen to all offers.

He wants to play for a contender.

He fueled speculation about a possible trade.

He brings a lot to the table.

His contract has hamstrung efforts to trade him.

Only a handful of teams can take on his contract.

And a player to be named later.

They want to showcase him.

He's on the trading block.

They will part ways at the end of the season.

He has a good grasp of their system.

Contracts

They exercised his option.

They will try to resign him before his contract is up.

He's a high priced free agent.

They're over the cap.

Free agency is killing the game.

We're working out the language.

They've gone the free agency route.

> They sacrificed their future with that trade.

It's a Tough Place to Play
Stadium Clichés

This park suits right handed hitters.

We need to **defend** our **home turf**.

In any other park, that's a home run.

They play in a bandbox.

They are road weary.

They have difficulty winning on the road.

It's a tough place to play.

It's not easy to go in there and come out with a win.

Home field/court/ice means everything.

He's on Fire
Hot Clichés

He has been red hot. – *Good Player*

He put out the fire. – *Baseball Pitcher*

This team is starting to ignite. – *Team*

He's packing heat. – *Baseball Pitcher*

This is a real barn burner. – *Game*

They burned another timeout. – *Football Offense*

He has a hot hand. – *Good Player*

He's on the hot seat. – *Bad Player*

He fired off the ball. – *Good Player*

He unleashed a scorcher. – *Baseball Pitcher*

They're really fired up. – *Team*

He's hot. – *Good Player*

He's swinging a hot bat.

– *Baseball Hitting*

1	AA	75
Sec	Row	Seat

We Look to Our Seniors

College Clichés

> Today is Andy Prince's last game along with his fellow seniors. *He doesn't have time to get sentimental* as *there's a bowl berth on the line*. Besides, they are playing their arch rival, MSU for *state bragging rights*. Regardless of the outcome, Andy's *had a stellar career* and *left his mark on the program*.

He was recruited by a number of top schools.

He's playing his last game as a <u>Wolverine</u>.
(fill in team)

He heads a strong freshman class.

He wants to come back for his senior year so he can earn his diploma.

The sanctions have taken their toll.

They are known as <u>linebacker</u> U.
(fill in position)

They're going to the big dance.

They have a number of starters returning from last season.

There is a bowl berth on the line.

It's tough to come right out of high school and play well.

This is the last time I'll put on a <u>Buckeye</u> uniform.
(fill in team)

This one is for bragging rights.

He's a blue chipper.

He has a future on Sundays.

That's a lot of ask of a freshman.

He's left his mark on the program.

He's turned the program around.

They're one and done.

He led them to a berth in the <u>Sugar Bowl</u>.
(fill in bowl)

This game has bowl implications.

This is the granddaddy of them all.

This is one of the most storied rivalries in college football.

1	AA	77
Sec	Row	Seat

Section 2

Are You Ready For Some Football?

Football Clichés

It Was a Hard Hitting Game
Game Clichés

It's my prediction that *the team with the fewest turnovers will win today's game.* The Raiders *bend but never break defense* has been *bailing them* out all season. On the *offensive side of the ball,* they have a *talented core of receivers* led by David Orr. Larry Smith, their tailback, is *a good north/south runner who usually makes the first guy miss.* Guy Davey is *your prototype 7 step drop back passer* who *likes to audible* at the line of scrimmage. *Their only glaring weakness is special teams which haven't been so special this year.*

Any team can win on any given Sunday.

The ball is just shy of the ___20___ yard line.
　　　　　　　　　　　　　　(fill in #)

They have good field position.

They got **stronger** as the **game** progressed.

The ball broke the vertical plane of the end zone.

The <u>wind</u> will be a factor.
　　(fill in factor)

They do a good job of concealing their weaknesses.

They came in well prepared.

They have a proven system.

This play is huge.

They're working with a short field.

It will be a game of field position.

The team that makes the fewest mistakes will win.

They got beat on both sides of the ball.

We took what they gave us.

They executed their game plan to perfection.

They came in with a well conceived game plan.

They've seized the momentum.

This game could come down to who has the ball last.

They're Back on Their Heels

Defense Clichés

They need to shut down their running/passing game.

They're putting pressure on the quarterback.

This game has become a defensive struggle.

The defense did its part.

The defense forced a number of turnovers.

They have a tendency to give up the big play.

Somebody needs to make a play.

He's a defensive stalwart.

The defense has stiffened.

They have a bend, but never break defense.

He has a real knack for the ball.

They're showing different defensive schemes.

The defense has been out on the field too long.

They disguise their defenses well.

He Put a Lick On Him
Tackling Clichés

He stuck him.

He stuffed him.

He got knocked into last week.

He unloaded on him.

He was hammered.

He put a big hit on him.

He cleaned his clock.

He blind-sided him.

He wrapped him up.

He got popped.

That was a bone crushing tackle.

That was a punishing hit.

You could feel that one all the way up here.

They're Moving the Ball at Will

Offense Clichés

They're moving the chains.

They have innovative offensive schemes.

A first down here and this game is over.

Their third down efficiency is not what it needs to be.

They're wearing them down.

They're mixing it up.

They are starting to open things up.

They have a number of players at the skilled positions.

They are not going to get too many opportunities like this.

They have spread the field.

They need a **big play** here.

It looks like a Chinese fire drill down there.

That play's going nowhere.

Row
Seat
Price

Section

They're trying to establish the run/pass.

They didn't fool anybody on that one.

They put the ball on the ground.

They **exposed** their **weaknesses** on defense.

They're moving the ball at will.

They don't want to go 3 and out.

That play was slow to develop.

They kept the **defense guessing.**

They're playing with reckless abandon.

They have trouble scoring in the red zone.

They can score from anywhere on the field.

2	BB	85
Sec	Row	Seat

He Heard Footsteps
Pass Coverage Clichés

If you live by the blitz, you die by the blitz.

They came after him.

That was a well-timed hit.

He made a good move on the ball.

How did they let him get loose?

Defensive backs need to have a short memory.

They blew their coverage.

That was a busted coverage.

He just sat back there.

He got a good break on the ball.

That was a coverage sack.

They're giving him too much cushion.

He covered him like a blanket.

He's their best cover man.

It's 3 Yards and a Cloud of Dust
Rushing Clichés

He's carrying the load.

He's their featured running back.

He almost broke it.

He makes the first guy miss.

He ran for daylight.

He has a lot of daylight in front of him.

He carried a truckload of defenders with him.

He's always a threat to go all the way.

It all starts up-front.

They're grinding out yardage.

They are playing running back by committee.

They methodically ground them down.

He could go all the way.

He can make you miss.

He gets a lot of YAC's.

He took it the distance.

He always seems to find the end zone.

He made something out of nothing.

He's a good north-south runner.

He Telegraphed That One
Quarterback Clichés

He liked what he saw.

He wasn't comfortable with what he saw.

He has a quick release.

He put the ball where only his receiver could catch it.

He looked off the receiver.

I bet he'd like to have that throw back.

He makes good decisions.

He went up top.

He's going deep.

He's throwing it underneath.

The most popular player on the team is the back-up quarterback.

He threw it up for a jump ball.

He's taking what the defense gives him.

He didn't put enough air under the ball.

He hit him in **stride**.

There's no quarterback controversy.

He's the closest thing to <u>Joe Montana</u> we've seen.
(fill in great player)

He threw that ball up for grabs.

2	BB	89
Sec	Row	Seat

He Had Him Beat

Receiving Clichés

He cradled the ball before it touched the ground.

He run precise routes.

He stretched out to catch that one.

He couldn't bring it in.

It hit him on the numbers.

The receiver did a good job of creating separation from the defender.

They've been having some protection problems.

He was a step away from breaking it.

He's their possession receiver.

He got both feet in.

He's a real game breaker.

Footballs are filling the air.

He Split the Uprights
Kicker Clichés

He kicked a dandy.

He's normally very reliable from that distance.

He got a lot of leg into that one.

This game will come down to special teams.

He got his toe into that one.

Their special teams have been anything but special.

This one has good hang time.

He has enough leg.

They're trying to ice the kicker.

2	BB	91
Sec	Row	Seat

Section 3

I Love This Game!

Basketball Clichés

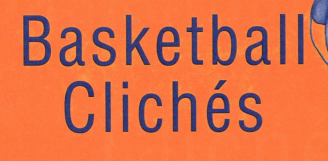

He Got Nothing But Net
Shooting Clichés

> It's Paulie Sipp's team as *the offense revolves around him*. He can *spot up for the open "J"* or take *the rock to the hoop*. He also has the ability *to hit from downtown*. Unfortunately, *his defense is suspect* as he's *easily beaten off the dribble*. Paulie's coach wants him *to learn to share the ball more* when *the defense collapses around him*. Also, his teammates have *a tendency to just stand around* when Paulie has the ball.

That's a forgiving rim.

He got the roll.

He gives them a good __10__ minutes off the bench.
(fill in #)

He's automatic.

He can really light up the scoreboard.

When the game is on the line, you want the ball in his hands.

He filled it up.

He likes the rock in his hand.

He had a quiet __22__ points tonight.
(fill in #)

He was rejected.

He sticks it.

He **forced** it **up**.

He got it to fall.

He kissed the glass.

He's been quiet so far.

He's perfect from the line/charity strip.

He tickled the twine.

He moves well without the ball.

He's giving them quality minutes.

He did a 360.

He swished it.

He's a street player.

He dropped one.

He got a good look.

He provides them with instant offense.

He's a good finisher.

He got the roll.

He's going to get his points.

He knocked it down.

You give him that shot and he'll make it all day.

You can't leave him that open.

He knows how to finish.

He hit it.

He's struggling at both ends of the floor.

He went coast to coast.

He had some real hang time.

He Shot It from Downtown

3 Pointer Clichés

He shot a rainmaker.

He shot a rainbow.

He drained a **3.**

It's raining **3's.**

He threw it up from beyond the arc.

He put up a **3** ball.

That's a triple.

He hit a trés.

He's hitting them from downtown.

He Owns the Glass
Rebounding Clichés

He can really elevate.

He controls the "no-fly" zone.

He plays **above the rim.**

He's a high riser.

He's got ups.

He controls the paint.

He really skyed for that rebound.

He crashed the boards.

He's really banging in there.

He's a force inside.

They are establishing a presence on the offensive glass.

He Got His Pocket Picked
Dribbling / Passing Clichés

Dribbling

He plays with his back to the basket.

He's good at penetrating.

He went strong to the hoop.

He put the ball on the floor.

He creates offense off the dribble.

He beat him off the dribble.

Passing

He dished it off.

They need to spread the ball around.

He gets everyone involved.

They need to share the ball more.

They made one pass too many.

He's pushing the ball up the floor.

It's Been a Game of Runs

Team Clichés

They need to make good decisions in transition.

They need to do a better job of denying him the ball.

They are contesting every shot.

They are making a run at them.

It's _____ team.
  (fill in player)

Everybody's just standing around.

They're giving them too many second chance opportunities.

They've got numbers.

They're **settling** for outside shots.

They are a perimeter shooting team.

They match up well size-wise.

They need to dominate the boards.

They like to pound the ball inside.

They're shooting the lights out.

They play an up-tempo game.

This game has turned into a track meet.

They have got to knock down their free throws.

There are a lot of mismatches out there.

They are helping each other out on defense.

They need to take a timeout here.

There's a lid on the basket.

3	CC	101
Sec	Row	Seat

Section 4

Play Ball!

Baseball Clichés

They Have Ducks on the Pond
Game Clichés

Randy Goode *has been their ace* for the last 3 years. He's *a strapping right-hander* who has *an arsenal of pitches*. Opponents need *to get to him early* as once *he gets into a rhythm,* he *will overpower hitters*. Today he *was aided by the long ball* as his number 5 and 6 batters hit *back to back tape measures jobs*. He was also helped by numerous White Sox miscues on the base paths. In the second inning, Ted Sanders was *caught napping at first base*. Then in the sixth, he was *caught in a rundown* after attempting to steal second.

It's a great day for a ball game.

They've batted around.

This is the rubber game of the series.

They'll trade an out for a run.

It's a real slugfest out there.

They could use an insurance run.

They had another scoreless stanza.

They like to play small ball.

He's a good bench jockey.

They whitewashed them.

He Fanned
Strikeout Clichés

He took a called 3rd strike.

He got rung up.

He was caught looking.

He was fooled on the pitch.

He whiffed on that one.

He looked like a rusty gate on that pitch.

The pitcher went right after him.

He went down swinging.

He Went the Distance

Pitcher Clichés

Positive Clichés

He has a lot of zip on the ball today.

He's got good throwing mechanics.

He's pitching a gem.

He's their ace.

He won't give him very much here.

They're playing pitch and catch.

He's overpowering the hitters.

They need to get to him early.

The pitching is ahead of the hitting at this point in the season.

He's been mowing down the hitters.

He threw a rocket.

He's pitching his Sunday best.

He helped his own cause.

He sent a message with that one.

He's really bringing it.

Negative Clichés

I bet he'd like to have that pitch back.

He put that pitch too far over the plate.

He's getting roughed up.

He needs to settle down.

He threw it into his wheelhouse.

He was knocked out of the box.

You can never have too much pitching.

4	DD	107
Sec	Row	Seat

He Ripped the Cover Off the Ball
Batter Clichés

He's leading the team in ribbies.

He's trying to bunt his way on.

He **hit it off** the end of the bat.

He's their clean-up hitter.

He hit a squibber.

He hit that ball squarely.

He hit a Baltimore chop.

He hit a Texas leaguer.

He **hit** for the **cycle.**

He made good contact.

He took a good rip.

He was all over that pitch.

He hit a frozen rope.

He's a different player between the lines.

He hit a bullet/rocket/laser/shot.

He hit the dirt.

He's trying to protect the runner.

He can't hit his own weight.

They took the bat out of his hands.

He gave himself up.

He's riding the pine.

He needs to move the runners along.

He chased a pitch out of the strike zone.

He's a Punch and Judy hitter.

He Tattooed That One

Home Run Clichés

He hit a couple of dingers today.

He hits them in bunches.

He hit it a country mile.

He really got ahold of that one.

He got all of it.

He crushed that one.

That one's going...going...gone.

Touch them all.

That one's out of here.

That was a tape measure job.

He sent the ball into orbit.

He launched a moon shot.

He tore into that one.

He teed off on that one.

They rely on the long ball.

He's swinging for the fences.

He got good wood on the ball.

That ball's long gone.

He really tagged that one.

He went yard.

You can kiss that one goodbye.

4	DD	111
Sec	Row	Seat

He Got a Good Jump
Base Running Clichés

They put the runners in motion.

He gives pitchers fits when he's on the base paths.

He got down the line in a hurry.

He was caught napping at first base.

That was a bush league play.

They put on the squeeze play.

That Was a Twin Killing
Double Play Clichés

They turned it over.

They turned two.

That double play was tailor-made.

That's an around the horn double play.

That was a bang-bang double play.

They got two for the price of one.

They did it the hard way.

He Showed Some Leather

Fielding Clichés

He threw it on a line.

The ball took a Sunday hop.

He made a circus catch.

He's a scrappy shortstop.

They've shortened up the infield.

They're strong up the middle.

That was a sparkling play.

He couldn't find the handle.

Section 5

He Shoots, He Scores

Hockey Clichés

They're Getting Beaten to the Puck

Team Clichés

> The Stars have been having trouble putting *the biscuit in the basket* during their *recent 4 game skid*. They have gone 5 periods without *turning on the red light*. Their best scoring opportunity was at the 11 minute mark of the second period when Shane Clark *attempted to go top shelf*. Goalie Patrick Kruse challenged him *by cutting down the angle*. Once again, *they failed to find the twine*.

Good things happen when you put the puck on the net.

They've gone into their defensive shell.

They have to find a way to put the puck in the net.

They're the hardest working line in hockey.

It's a **fast ice** tonight.

They skated to a __2-2__ tie.
(fill in score)

The bodies are flying.

They're changing on the fly.

The Stanley Cup goes through <u>Detroit</u>.
(fill in team)

They'll need to go upstairs to review this goal.

They're **digging** for the puck.

I went to a fight and a hockey game broke out.

He Stood On His Head
Goalie Clichés

He's played well between the pipes.

He stoned him.

He robbed him.

He gave up a soft goal.

He pitched a shutout.

They pulled the goalie.

The goal posts are a goalie's best friend.

He Put the Biscuit in the Basket
Scoring Clichés

He shot it through the 5 hole.

He went top shelf.

He went upstairs.

He beat the goalie.

He found the twine.

He turned the red light on.

He found the back of the net.

He lit the lamp.

That's a **red light special**.

He Split the Defense
Player Clichés

He iced the puck

He took a run at him.

He fanned on the shot.

He's tied up in the corner.

He put it right on his stick.

He stood him up.

He dumped the puck into the zone.

It's a frozen puck.

He's got the puck on a string.

Section 5

5 Sec | EE Row | 119 Seat

Section 6

He Teed It Up

Golf Clichés

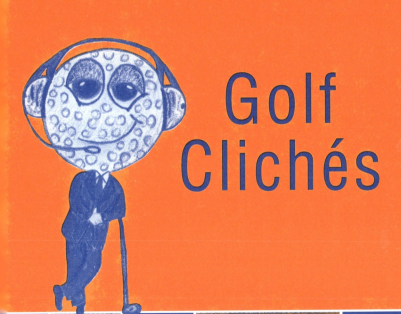

He Won't Be Happy With That Shot
Shot Clichés

We're here at the 18th hole at Augusta. Unlike the second round, *today's playing conditions have just been spectacular.* Roger Wood *just teed up the ball* and *hit a monster drive.* I think *he is going to be happy with that shot* as *he hit it on the screws.* Despite the fact *the greens are rock hard,* his *ball landed pin high.* This is *a very makeable putt* and if *he drains it,* he'll *be atop the leader board heading into the final round.*

The ball is pin high.

He's in the beach.

I believe the ball has found the water.

That was a monster drive.

Nice putt, Alice.

That shot's all over it.

He's got a **bad case** of the **yips**.

He cut that shot in there from left to right.

That putt took tremendous courage.

This is a very makeable putt.

He hit it on the screws.

That putt is a big bender.

He **crushed** that drive.

That shot had a lot of juice on it.

You drive for show and putt for dough.

He really teed off on that one.

He came up short.

Get in the hole!

That putt is inside the leather.

He needs this shot to save par.

That's about the best he could have done from there.

6	FF	123
Sec	Row	Seat

Here's Making His Charge

Tournament/Course Clichés

He didn't make the cut.

The greens are rock hard.

The greens are as fast as ice.

That is a sucker pin.

The pins are tucked into some tight places.

He's the leader in the clubhouse.

He's the best player never to have won a major.

The tournament starts on the back nine on Sunday.

There's still a lot of golf to be played.

There's a logjam atop the leader board.

Section 7

Game, Set, Match

Tennis Clichés

He Bageled Him
Player Clichés

He's playing to the crowd.

He is the future of U.S. tennis.

He tuned him.

He dusted him.

He's the puppet master.

He's got his opponent on a string.

He's a human backboard.

He didn't break a sweat until shaking hands.

He's an all court player.

He's a dirt baller.

He's hot, repaint the lines.

He dusted the lines.

He's a retriever.

He's running down everything.

He Served Up an Ace
Shot Clichés

After 3 days of rain, it's perfect tennis weather *for this long anticipated Wimbledon final* between Andy Crowell and Mats Schwager. Crowell, considered *the future of U.S. tennis,* has been ranked number one for 23 consecutive weeks. He has *been bombing his serves* all afternoon and *bageled Schwager in the first set* which took just under 30 minutes to complete. He has *been dusting the lines* in the second set and *has barely broken a sweat.*

He hooked him.

He likes to chip and charge.

He likes to **dice** and **slice**.

He took the air out of the ball.

The lob did the job.

He gripped it and ripped it.

He has a cannonball serve.

He bombed in his serve.

He knifed a volley.

He served a can opener.

Sec	Row	Seat
7	GG	127

Section 8

This Game Will Be Won In the Trenches

Sports Cliché Origins

It's a War Out There
Military Clichés

> The Colts have *an explosive offense* and have been *marching down the field* at will. They've been beating their opponents *at the point of attack* led by Tom Henson who has *a cannon for an arm*. Clearly, the Seahawks *are shell shocked* by what's happening.

Everybody's gunning for us. – *Team*

They have an **uphill battle**. – *Team*

The defense will try to thwart the aerial assault. – *Football Defense*

He changed his cadence. – *Quarterback*

They're winning the battle of the boards. – *Basketball Rebound*

He shoots like a sniper. – *Basketball Shooting*

He has a howitzer/rifle/cannon/shot gun for an arm. – *Quarterback*

We need to win the <u>turnover battle</u>. – *Game*
(fill in factor)

They have an excellent passing attack. – *Football Offense*

It was a **hard fought** game. – *Game*

They're in everyone's cross-hairs. – *Team*

They boast a well-balanced attack. – *Football Offense*

He's in the line of fire. – *Good Player*

He fought for extra yardage. – *Football Rushing*

They're showing blitz. – *Football Defense*

They're shell shocked by what's happening. – *Team*

He exploded to the basket. – *Basketball Dribbling*

To the victors go the spoils. – *Team*

He has an arsenal of pitches. – *Baseball Pitcher*

He's leading the charge. – *Good Player*

They have an explosive offense. – *Football Offense*

They are marching down the field. – *Football Offense*

He's a real juggernaut. – *Good Player*

They have an attacking defense. – *Football Defense*

They have many weapons in their arsenal. – *Team*

He beat him at the point of attack.

– *Football Defense*

8	HH	131
Sec	Row	Seat

We Shot Ourselves in the Foot

Wild West Clichés

The Pirates hope to put enough runners on base to enable *their big guns* to come to bat this inning. After *riding the pine* for most of the season, Eli Abrams pinch hit with a runner on first. He hit *a shot into the hole* that was *speared by the shortstop* who quickly threw to first, doubling off Skip Bartlet. What *a bang-bang play*. The next batter struck out ending the threat and *saddled Chuck Kess with his third consecutive loss*.

Gun Clichés

He's gun shy out there. — *Bad Player*

He's under the gun. — *Bad Player*

He has an itchy trigger finger. — *Quarterback*

They withstood their best shot. — *Game*

He's in **shotgun formation**. — *Quarterback*

He's a real gunslinger. — *Quarterback*

Their **big guns** are coming to bat. — *Baseball Batter*

That was a bang bang play. — *Baseball Fielding*

He **gunned down** the runner. — *Baseball Fielding*

He pulled the trigger. — *Good Player*

This game has become a real shootout. — *Game*

They're going to take a shot at it. — *Football Game*

They're heading into next week's showdown. — *Big Game*

They dodged a bullet. – *Team*

They took a shot down the field. – *Football Game*

They have a run and gun offense. – *Football Offense*

Horse Clichés

They rode their defense to victory. – *Football Defense*

He's riding the pine. – *Bad Player*

They saddled them with another loss. – *Team*

He horse collared him. – *Football Tackling*

He's on his horse. – *Speed*

His players have a lot of free rein. – *Coach*

They mounted a comeback. – *Team*

Other Clichés

The wheels are falling off the wagon. – *Team*

This is a real pitcher's duel. – *Baseball Pitching*

We're still in the hunt. – *Team*

> They are the team everyone's shooting for.
>
> – *Good Team*

They Need to Right the Ship

Nautical Clichés

With Mel Rathburn *at the helm,* there is hope that he *can turn the ship around.* He's only *been their skipper* for 1 month, but has already brought in some new players *to anchor the defense.* Hopefully, that *will bail the team out* of their current doldrums.

He sank the putt. – *Golf*

They're cruising on offense. – *Football Offense*

They need to turn the ship around. – *Team*

He's at the helm. – *Coach*

He's a showboat. – *Bad Player*

That took the wind out of their sails. – *Team*

This team is sinking fast. – *Team*

They bailed him out. – *Team*

He anchors the defense. – *Good Player*

The ball sailed into the end zone. – *Football Kicking*

He's been their skipper for many years. – *Baseball Game*

They weathered the storm. – *Team*

They come at you in waves. – *Team*

They need to batten down the hatches. – *Team*

He's Pleading His Case
Legal Clichés

Law Clichés

That's his patented jumper. — *Basketball Shooting*

The ruling on the field stands. — *Officiating*

He was denied. — *Bad Player*

They made judicious use of their timeouts. — *Football Offense*

He served notice. — *Good Player*

His record speaks for itself. — *Good Player*

He gave up a number of innocent hits. — *Baseball Pitcher*

Crime Clichés

He stole that one on the pitcher. — *Baseball Base Running*

He was mugged. — *Officiating*

He handcuffed him on that pitch. — *Baseball Pitching*

That was highway robbery. — *Good Player*

They stole this game. — *Team*

They solved him. — *Good Player*

> The jury is still out on him.
> — *Bad Player*

8	HH	135
Sec	Row	Seat

He Did His Homework
School Clichés

Coach Art Keefer and his star right winger, Sheldon Ladd, *have not been on the same page* since the start of the season. Keefer's *coaching style is old school* and has *not played well* with the younger players on the team. The fact that Ladd *missed several key assignments* and made some dumb plays has only created more animosity between the two. *This could be all she wrote* for Ladd's *tenure with the team.*

They've been having a storybook season. – *Team*

They passed this test in flying colors. – *Team*

You can't teach this. – *Good Player*

We'll keep playing hard until we're mathematically eliminated. – *Team*

He's the dean of the secondary. – *Football Coverage*

Someone missed his assignment. – *Bad Player*

He's putting on a clinic. – *Good Player*

He made good reads. – *Quarterback*

That's all she wrote. – *Game*

The handwriting is on the wall. – *Team*

His coaching style is old school. – *Coach*

His tenure with the team may be coming to an end. – *Bad Player*

They withstood the test. – *Team*

School is out. – *Game*

This will be their most difficult test. – *Team*

These players have a lot of history. – *Fighting*

That was a textbook play. – *Team*

He schooled him. – *Good Player*

They read him like a book. – *Team*

It's all academic now. – *Game*

He wrote the book on <u>bunting</u>. – *Good Player*
(fill in skill)

They have got to answer here. – *Team*

You can put this one in the book. – *Game*

They brought their "A" game today. – *Team*

They are not on the same page. – *Team*

He's a student of the game. – *Good Player*

They've been well schooled. – *Team*

We were thoroughly outclassed today. – *Team*

He's in a class by himself.

– *Good Player*

8	HH	137
Sec	Row	Seat

He's Paying Dividends
Money Clichés

Randy Geha, the Devil Ray's veteran catcher, *has been working the count.* Here comes the payoff pitch. Tim Jeremy, the Cardinals' closer, threw a fastball down the middle and Randy *made him pay for it.* Eventually, they sent 8 batters to the plate and clearly *made a statement* by taking a 6 run lead. *This one's money in the bank.*

That was a costly penalty. – *Officiating*

We can't afford another loss. – *Team*

Here's the payoff pitch. – *Baseball Pitching*

The players need to buy into it. – *Coach*

They're nickeling and dimeing them to death. – *Quarterback*

He's made a modest contribution. – *Good Player*

They squandered another opportunity. – *Team*

They're buying some time. – *Team*

They can't buy a basket. – *Basketball Shooting*

They don't have the luxury of a <u>deep bullpen</u>. – *Team*
(fill in anything)

He increased his stock. – *Good Player*

We got contributions from a lot of people. – *Team*

He took it to pay dirt. – *Football Offense*

He made them pay for it. – *Good Player*

He's money. – *Good Player*

They have a stingy defense. – *Team*

I have to give them all the credit. – *Team*

He's a rags to riches story. – *Good Player*

He's worth the price of admission. – *Good Player*

This one's money in the bank. – *Game*

They need to **capitalize** here. – *Game*

They have to cash in here. – *Game*

Their offense has been very charitable today.

– *Football Offense*

We Got the Monkey Off Our Backs

Animal Clichés

The Chiefs were in a real dogfight today. John Kush, their rookie quarterback, has *had trouble holding on to the pigskin,* but was *still barking out signals* in the 4th quarter. He dropped back to pass, but got hit just as he released the ball, causing him *to throw up a wounded duck.* The ball was intercepted and run back for a touchdown making Kush *the game's goat.* Needless to say, *this brought the boo birds out.*

They are playing this game at a snail's pace. – *Team*

The zebras are calling a tight game. – *Officiating*

The **boo birds** are out. – *Fans*

They've been underdogs all season. – *Team*

They have been benevolent with the pigskin. – *Football Offense*

He was the game's goat. – *Bad Player*

They're playing like chickens with their heads cut off. – *Team*

I'd like to be a fly on the wall of that locker room. – *Team*

They came roaring back. – *Team*

He threw up a wounded duck. – *Quarterback*

He was a sitting duck back there. – *Quarterback*

He threw him a gopher ball. – *Baseball Pitcher*

He's barking out signals. – *Quarterback*

They've gotten them back on their haunches. – *Football Offense*

It's a game of cat and mouse. – *Game*

They're in for a real dog fight. – *Team*

He's in the coach's dog house.

– *Coach*

8	HH	141
Sec	Row	Seat

They're a Blue Collar Team

Business Clichés

They own them. – *Team*

His pitches are really working for him. – *Baseball Pitcher*

He retired the side in order. – *Baseball Pitcher*

They need to manufacture some runs. – *Baseball Game*

They need to step up their run production. – *Baseball Game*

They have to do a better job of protecting the ball. – *Bad Team*

He's a franchise player. – *Good Player*

They're making a statement. – *Team*

They're dictating the tempo of the game. – *Team*

He's working the count. – *Baseball Batter*

He'll file this one away for future reference. – *Good Player*

It was another day at the office. – *Team*

We took care of business. – *Team*

We have some **unfinished business** with them. – *Team*

<u>Basketball</u> is a business. – *Front Office*
(fill in sport)

They Play In Your Face
Parts of the Body Clichés

> Carl Franklin *has his game face on*. All season long, he's *carried the Knicks on his back*. This game has been *a real nail biter* with the victor *having a leg up* on winning the division title. Unfortunately, *it's gut check time* which has been New York's *achilles heel all season long*. They continue *to break their fans' hearts*.

Eyes

He read the eyes of the quarterback. – *Football Coverage*

That was a real **eye opener.** – *Game*

That was a seeing eye single. – *Baseball Batter*

That ball had eyes. – *Baseball Batter*

Heart

They're playing with a lot of heart. – *Team*

He's the heart and soul of the team. – *Good Player*

They played their hearts out. – *Team*

He has the heart of a champion. – *Good Player*

Legs and Feet

We left with our tails between our legs. – *Team*

He kept his feet moving. – *Football Offense*

The winner will have a leg up. – *Team*

That has been their Achilles heel all season. – *Team*

Hands and Arms

They need to get their hands on the ball. – *Team*

That plays into the <u>Rangers</u> hands. – *Team*
(fill in opponent)

Their fate is in their own hands. – *Team*

It's clear that the right hand doesn't know what the left hand is doing. – *Team*

He's got the batters eating out of his hand. – *Baseball Pitcher*

There's a lot of finger pointing going on. – *Team*

Torso

He's not afraid to give up his body. – *Good Player*

Everything rests on his shoulders. – *Good Player*

Their backs are against the wall. – *Team*

This team needs to do some soul searching. – *Team*

It's gut check time. – *Game*

Face and Head

They're going for the jugular. – *Team*

He has his game face on. – *Good Player*

He's a real cerebral player. – *Good Player*

They snatched a victory from the jaws of defeat. – *Good Team*

He's a head case. – *Bad Player*

There are a lot of mind games going on. – *Game*

He gets in your face. – *Good Player*

They missed it by the nose of the football. – *Football Offense*

There's a lot of head scratching going on. – *Team*

They ran the ball down our throats. – *Football Rushing*

We have nothing to hang our heads about. – *Team*

He changes the complexion of the entire team. – *Good Player*

> They're showing some new wrinkles on offense.
>
> – *Football Offense*

They Couldn't Have Scripted It Better
Entertainment / Electricity Clichés

Entertainment

He has a good supporting cast. — *Team*

The big stage doesn't bother him. — *Rookie*

They're back on the NFL's grand stage. — *Team*
(fill in league)

He's a good gauge of talent. — *Coach*

He likes to play on the stage with the brightest lights. — *Good Player*

He's putting on a show. — *Good Player*

It's showtime! — *Team*

Electricity

The stadium is charged with electricity. — *Fans*

We shocked the world. — *Team*

This has been a real shocker. — *Game*

He's a lightning rod for criticism. — *Bad Player*

He's a real powerhouse out there. — *Good Player*

You can feel the electricity. — *Fans*

That play electrified the crowd. — *Fans*

That play galvanized the team. — *Team*

It's Back to the Drawing Board

Artist Clichés

They're a work in progress. – *Team*

He's a knuckleball artist. – *Baseball Pitcher*

They're putting the finishing touches on this victory. – *Game*

They ran it just the way it was drawn up. – *Game*

He painted the corner. – *Baseball Pitcher*

He drew the foul. – *Officiating*

They etched out a victory.

– *Victory*

Sec	Row	Seat
8	HH	147

They're Playing for All the Marbles
Hobby Clichés

Play Clichés

There's a real tug of war going on down there. – *Game*

They have the building blocks in place. – *Team*

They still need a few more pieces to the puzzle. – *Team*

It's a chess match going on out there. – *Game*

It was a seesaw battle all the way. – *Game*

Fishing Clichés

He's trade bait. – *Front Office*

There is so much on the line today. – *Game*

He picked up the slack. – *Good Player*

He laid it on the line. – *Good Player*

He fell for it hook, line, and sinker. – *Bad Player*

You Can Stick a Fork in Him
Food Clichés

Having been out of the pennant race since August, the Indians have *relished the role of spoiler.* Unfortunately, in the 9th inning today, their top reliever threw a *meatball down the middle* of the plate. Chad Deitch hit an opposite field double *setting the table* for Mike Samuels, their clean-up hitter. The Indians certainly *have something cooking here.*

It's garbage time. – *Basketball Game*

He got stuffed. – *Bad Player*

He's getting his licks up there. – *Baseball Batter*

The crowd is egging them on. – *Fan*

They are toast. – *Team*

He's hamming it up for the crowd. – *Good Player*

That's the icing on the cake. – *Game*

He had to eat the ball. – *Quarterback*

They laid an egg out there. – *Team*

---

8 **HH** **149**
Sec Row Seat

He hit him in the bread basket. – *Quarterback*

That was a meatball down the middle. – *Baseball Pitcher*

He got the meat of the bat on the ball. – *Baseball Batter*

He's been seeing a steady diet of curve balls. – *Baseball Batter*
(fill in pitch)

There's a good crop of players in this year's draft. – *Rookies*

He put a lot of mustard on the ball. – *Baseball Pitcher*

They've got him in a pickle. – *Baseball Running*

He's their bread and butter. – *Good Player*

He shaked and baked. – *Basketball Dribbling*

They need a win to starve off elimination. – *General Team*

He held the football like a loaf of bread. – *Football Rushing*

He bit on the fake. – *Football Coverage*

He has ice water in his veins. – *Pressure*

He's a flash in the pan. – *Bad Player*

They relish the role of spoiler. – *Team*

That's a can of corn. – *Baseball Fielding*

He didn't cut it. – *Bad Player*

They're missing a key ingredient. – *Team*

We made them eat their words. – *Team*

He set the table. – *Baseball Batter*

He's cherry picking. – *Basketball Shooting*

The ref gave them some home cooking on that call.

– *Officiating*

8	HH	151
Sec	Row	Seat

He's All Washed Up

Water Clichés

They had a __6__ run outburst. – *Baseball Hitting*
(fill in #)

He's a spray hitter. – *Baseball Batter*

He stepped in the bucket. – *Baseball Batter*

He drained the putt. – *Golf*

That ended a __5:20__ minute scoring drought. – *Basketball Game*
(fill in #)

Their lead just evaporated. – *Basketball Game*

The fans are doing the wave. – *Fans*

He flushed it. – *Basketball Shooting*

The tide is turning. – *Game*

They went to the well once too often. – *Team*

He Threw Up a Brick
Construction Clichés

Building Clichés

They're building the franchise around him. – *Good Player*

He's the cornerstone of this team. – *Good Player*

They have a lot of real estate to work with. – *Football Offense*

He knows how to handle the lumber. – *Baseball Batter*

He nailed it. – *Good Player*

They are in a rebuilding mode. – *Team*

He has a blueprint for success. – *Coach*

He's the **architect** of their **defense**. – *Coach*

He's coming in to nail down the victory. – *Baseball Pitcher*

He has a lot of fences to mend. – *Bad Player*

We ran into a buzz saw today. – *Team*

He's starting to build something good here. – *Coach*

8	HH	153
Sec	Row	Seat

House Clichés

They shut/slammed/closed the door on them. – *Team*

They have a lot of room to operate in. – *Football Offense*

They went back door. – *Basketball Shooting*

He stayed home. – *Football Defense*

He needs to play within the framework of the <u>offense</u>. – *Good Player*
(fill in factor)

They've got a lock on this one. – *Game*

They are perpetual cellar dwellers. – *Baseball Game*

They're knocking on the door. – *Game*

He took it to the house. – *Good Player*

Hole Clichés

They have one last ditch chance. – *Game*

We need to plug some holes. – *Team*

They have a big void to fill. – *Team*

He hit the hole. – *Football Rushing*

He hit the ball in the hole. – *Baseball Batter*

He went to the hole. – *Basketball Shooting*

The batter is digging in. – *Baseball Hitting*

We dug ourselves into a hole. – *Team*

They dug deep. – *Team*

They're digging for the puck. – *Hockey Skating*

They have a lot of holes to fill.

– *Team*

8	HH	155
Sec	Row	Seat

He's Nursing an Injury
Medical Clichés

They need to lick their wounds. – *Team*

They are sitting in the nosebleed section. – *Fan*

He's playing out of his mind. – *Good Player*

They used a **suffocating defense**. – *Team*

They scratched out a run. – *Baseball Hitting*

They're nursing a __4__ point lead. – *Game*
(fill in #)

That was an ill-fated play. – *Game*

He took an **ill-advised** shot. – *Basketball Shooting*

They need to take better care of the ball. – *Team*

Row
Seat
Price

Section
8

He's been unconscious. – *Good Player*

That's got to hurt. – *Football Defense*

We've taken some lumps. – *Team*

They collapsed in the 4th quarter. – *Game*

It's nothing that a win won't cure. – *Team*

We need to stop the bleeding. – *Team*

That was a real back breaker. – *Game*

He coughed up the puck/ball. – *Bad Player*

He's been plagued by injuries throughout his career.

– *Injuries*

8	HH	157
Sec	Row	Seat

It's Do or Die

Life and Death Clichés

Life Clichés

He has a new lease on life. – *Veteran*

He's running for his life. – *Quarterback*

They **live** and **die** by the 3. – *Basketball 3 Pointer*

This drive has been kept alive by <u>penalties</u>. – *Football Offense*
(fill in event)

They've got some life left. – *End of Game*

They're showing signs of life. – *Game*

He's staying alive. – *Baseball Batter*

Their playoff hopes are still alive. – *Team*

Death Clichés

He attempted a suicide squeeze. – *Baseball Batter*

They never say die. – *Team*

They killed the penalty. – *Hockey Skating*

They have a murderous schedule. – *Team*

Speed kills. – *Speed*

He kicked it in the coffin corner. – *Kicking*

Turnovers will kill you. – *Football Offense*

It all comes down to execution. – *Game*

He put a dagger in their hearts. – *Good Player*

They need to kill some clock. – *Clock*

They put the nail in the coffin. – *Defeat*

That <u>call</u> will come back to haunt them. – *Team*
(fill in anything)

That was a heart stopping finish. – *Game*

They need more of a killer instinct.

– *Team*

8	HH	159
Sec	Row	Seat

He Threw Up a Hail Mary

Religious Clichés

They've resurrected themselves after a poor start. — *Team*

He atoned for his earlier mistake. — *Good Player*

He's being given a baptism by fire. — *Good Rookie*

He committed a cardinal sin. — *Bad Player*

They got their signals crossed. — *Team*

He threw up a prayer. — *Bad Player*

They failed to convert. — *Team*

They're playing like a team possessed. — *Team*

He's Seeing the Ball Well
Sense Clichés

Sight Clichés

We were caught looking ahead. — *Defeat*

Hindsight is always 20/20. — *Defeat*

I've seen stranger things happen. — *Game*

They have been overlooked. — *Team*

They lost sight of him. — *Football Receiving*

We're seeing a different player today. — *Good Player*

He looked off the receiver. — *Quarterback*

He made a great no look pass. — *Basketball Passing*

He sees the entire floor. — *Basketball Passing*

They look good on paper. — *Team*

He's looking over the defense. — *Quarterback*

> He doesn't like what he sees.
> — *Quarterback*

Sec 8 | Row HH | Seat 161

They've got the championship within their sights. – *Team*

The defense is giving them different looks. – *Football Defense*

That play really didn't look like much. – *Hockey Game*

They're getting some good open looks. – *Basketball Shooting*

The ref lost sight of the ball/puck. – *Officiating*

You can see the scared look in their eyes. – *Team*

Sound Clichés

We were beaten soundly. – *Defeat*

They are fundamentally sound. – *Team*

He silenced his critics. – *Good Player*

They are going to hear about that one in the locker room. – *Coach*

They should always keep playing until the whistle sounds. – *Officiating*

You could hear a pin drop. – *Unhappy Fans*

You could hear that hit from up here. – *Football Tackling*

They played hard until the gun/horn/buzzer sounded. – *Team*

Touch Clichés

You have to feel good about today's performance. – *Victory*

He gave them all they could handle. – *Good Player*

I have no bad feelings towards them. – *Front Office*

They handled everything that was thrown at them. – *Victory*

He could feel the blitz coming. – *Quarterback*

He has a good touch on the ball. – *Quarterback*

He has a shooter's touch. – *Basketball Shooting*

He needs a lot of touches. – *Good Player*

The crowd is letting them know how they feel. – *Unhappy Fans*

They're having trouble holding on to the pigskin. – *Football Offense*

The Drive Stalled
Travel Clichés

Auto Clichés

He drove them down the field. — *Quarterback*

This was a good tune up for our next game. — *Victory*

He put on the brakes. — *Good Player*

They look like they ran out of gas. — *Team*

Their **offense** has been sputtering. — *Team*

They're in the driver's seat now. — *Team*

There's a lot riding on this game. — *Big Game*

They're running on all cylinders. — *Team*

He's a real spark plug. — *Good Player*

They're driving deep into <u>Steeler</u> territory. — *Football Offense*
(fill in team)

They have a high powered offense. — *Football Offense*

They came out flat. – *Bad Team*

He has a bad wheel. – *Injury*

He misfired. – *Quarterback*

He caught it in traffic. – *Football Receiving*

He was driven out of bounds. – *Football Defense*

Trip Clichés

We don't have an easy road. – *Team*

It just shows how far we've come. – *Team*

It's been a long road. – *Team*

He gave the ball a ride. – *Baseball Hitting*

All the losses are starting to take their toll. – *Team*

We've been gearing up for this game.

– *Rivalry*

The teams are headed in opposite directions. – *Team*

This team could go far into the playoffs. – *Team*

They're headed in the **right direction**. – *Team*

He drove one out of here. – *Baseball Home Run*

There was some traveling music. – *Officiating*

The team lacks direction. – *Bad Team*

They're in it for the long haul. – *Good Team*

They are not a good road team. – *Bad Team*

They are road weary. – *Team*

We ran into a roadblock today. – *Defeat*

It will be a long plane/bus ride back home. – *Defeat*

He's on a mission. – *Good Player*

He Has Some Big Shoes to Fill

Clothing Clichés

Row Seat Price — Section 8

He was stripped of the ball. – *Bad Player*

They put their pants on one leg at a time. – *Team*

I have to tip my hat to them. – *Defeat*

The teams are sizing up one another. – *Game*

He's in street clothes. – *Injury*

The pocket is collapsing around him. – *Quarterback*

He made a fine shoestring catch. – *Baseball Fielding*

He's a good fit for us. – *Good Player*

He has good pocket presence. – *Quarterback*

He was faked out of his jock. – *Bad Player*

They've got to go to the rack more. – *Basketball Shooting*

He was left hanging out to dry. – *Bad Team*

He's pressing. – *Bad Player*

He was clotheslined. – *Football Tackling*

He was all over him like a cheap suit.

– *Good Player*

8 Sec | **HH** Row | **167** Seat

He Beat All Odds

Gambling / Magic Clichés

Gambling

When the chips are down, they play their best. — *Team*

It looks like their luck's run out. — *Game*

He's a real gambler. — *Good Player*

They always have a chance. — *Team*

They are the odds on favorite. — *Team*

They're going to roll the dice on this one. — *Game*

The odds are stacked against them. — *Team*

We need to just let the chips fall where they may. — *Team*

They don't want to take any chances here. — *Game*

Nobody gave us a chance. — *Victory*

They hit the jackpot with that one. — *Game*

Magic

He's up to his old tricks. – *Good Player*

He went into his bag of tricks. – *Good Player*

He pulled that one out of his hat. – *Good Player*

I wonder what other tricks he has up his sleeve. – *Good Player*

He doesn't miss a trick.

– *Good Player*

8	HH	169
Sec	Row	Seat

Section 9

He's In Our Corner

Clichés in the Mainstream

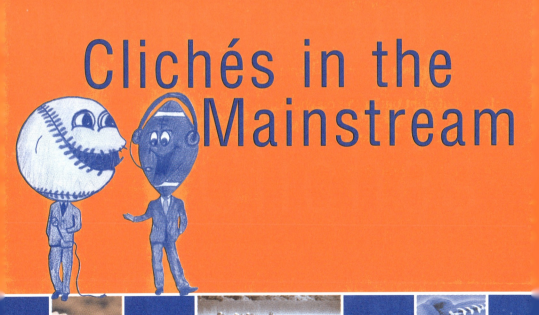

He's On His Game

All Sports

He's picking his spots.

It's a **toss-up.**

They called his number.

He's a clutch player.

He made a rookie mistake.

It's time to lace them up.

They have our number.

He's at the top of his game.

He came to play.

He's a team player.

It's a whole new ball game.

They're the team to **beat.**

We need to play them one at a time.

He took it right out of the playbook.

They need to settle the score.

The ball didn't bounce our way.

He Goes the Extra Yard
Football

They're piling it on.

He came up short.

He took the ball and ran with it.

He's in the zone.

They have a good game plan.

It's time to punt.

He went over the top.

We want to play on a level field.

9	II	173
Sec	Row	Seat

They Put On a Full Court Press

Basketball

It's crunch time.

It's a slam dunk.

He's their number one option.

They're going **one on one**.

He scored major points with that one.

He's a big shot.

They have a thin bench.

He Stepped Up
Baseball

He hit a home run.

That was a major league move.

He's in a league of his own.

He dropped the ball.

He plays the field.

It ain't over til the fat lady sings.

He needs to step up to the plate.

9 | II | 175
Sec | Row | Seat

They're Running On All Cylinders
Auto Racing

They are positioned to take the pole position.

He's running on fumes.

He's shifting gears.

He's revving up.

He **kicked** it into **high** gear.

He's headed into the last lap.

We need to get into gear.

He Went Wire to Wire
Horse Racing

They stumbled out of the gate.

The stakes are high.

They're heading down the home stretch.

He took the lead right out of the gate.

It's a 2 horse race.

He's a long shot.

He's off to the races.

This one's for all the money.

He has to be considered the dark horse.

They Went Toe to Toe

Boxing

They are on the mat.

They have them on the ropes.

He's up against the ropes.

He answered the bell.

They're delivering the knock-out punch.

They're a good one-two punch.

He didn't pull any punches.

He's down for the count.

He threw in the towel.

He Raised the Bar

Track

He went the distance.

He's in it for the long run.

He's hitting his stride.

He's the front runner.

We're in it for the long run.

He jumped the gun.

He has the inside track.

Section 10

Can You Get 110%?

Sports Cliché Quiz

Sports Cliché Quiz

Questions

How knowledgeable are you on clichés? Well, here's your chance *to bring your "A" game to the table* and show *you're the real deal*. Fill in the blanks with the appropriate word or words to complete the cliché. The correct answers along with how you scored are on pages 190-192.

1. They found a _____ to win.

2. Everyone has been _____ us out.

3. They played well down the _____.

4. They went _____ to wire.

5. We're not going to _____ yet.

6. We don't have any _____.

7. They _____ it more than we did.

8. Their worst _____ came true.

9. You make your own _____.

10. We'll keep playing hard until we're _____ eliminated.

11. It's only a matter of _____ before they score.

12. He wants to show that he _____ in this league.

13. They are letting them _____ around.

14. They put the _____ in the coffin.

15. We need to win at all _____.

16. They're just _____ to be here.

17. We played _____ game.

18. They got the _____ off their back.

19. They have a big _____ to fill.

20. We need to _____ it up.

21. We _____ ourselves in the foot.

22. That was an ill-advised _____.

23. He wasn't able to get into a _____.

24. He needs more _____ experience.

25. He committed a _____ sin.

26. He's a _____ artist.

27. That's the _____ point on a sterling career.

28. They want to _____ it over.

29. The front office is _____ him.

30. I'm more _____ of this team than any other.

31. They're _____ not to lose.

32. He's clearly not _____ with his team's play.

33. The referees are _____ them play.

34. That was a good _____ call.

35. We have a lot of _____ and bruises.

36. He has a good _____ of their system.

37. They used good _____ management.

38. They ran it just the way it was _____ _____.

39. They have a lot of _____ in their arsenal.

40. They _____ the storm.

41. The wheels are _____ off the wagon.

42. That was a _____ bang play.

42. This is a real pitcher's _____.

44. They are not on the same _____.

45. This one's _____ in the bank.

46. We have some _____ business with them.

47. His _____ speaks for itself.

48. The _____ birds are out.

49. He put a _____ in their hearts.

50. He got the _____ of the bat on the ball.

51. This game has _____ implications.

52. This game has become a _____ struggle.

53. That was a _____ crushing tackle.

54. He didn't _____ on the fake.

55. They're _____ on the door.

56. They're playing with reckless _____.

57. They're grinding out _____.

58. The defense will try to _____ the aerial assault.

59. They are playing running back by _____.

60. He makes the first guy _____.

61. He's always a _____ to go all the way.

62. He was left hanging out to _____.

63. He's taking what the _____ gives him.

64. He has good _____ presence.

65. Their special teams have been anything but _____.

66. It's impossible to totally _____ him.

67. He _____ the twine.

68. He's struggling at both _____ of the floor.

69. He lost the _____ on the ball.

70. They need to share the _____ more.

71. He's giving them _____ minutes.

72. There's a _____ on the basket.

73. That was a good piece of _____.

74. They have _____ on the pond.

75. They could use an _____ run.

76. They need to get to him _____.

77. He handcuffed him on that _____.

78. He sent a _____ with that one.

79. He hit a frozen _____.

80. He can't hit his own _____.

81. They took the _____ out of his hands.

82. He needs to _____ the runners along.

83. You can _____ that one goodbye.

84. He got good _____ on the ball.

85. He was caught _____ at first base.

86. That was a _____ league play.

87. They're _____ up the middle.

88. That's an around the horn _____ _____.

89. He gave up a _____ goal.

90. The goal posts are a goalie's _____ _____.

91. He _____ it through the 5 hole.

92. He dumped the puck into the _____.

93. He's the best player never to have won a _____.

94. He _____ it between the screws.

95. There's a _____ on top of the leader board.

96. The tournament _____ on the back nine on Sunday.

97. He _____ up an ace.

98. We have to _____ up to the next _____.

99. They've done well right out of the _____.

100. They need to pick up the _____.

101. They're running on all _____.

102. It was a total _____ effort.

103. They're playing out of _____.

104. It's a _____ place to play.

105. You can feel the _____ changing.

106. This game is our _____.

107. They came out and made _____.

108. They are _____ the tempo of the game.

109. They know how to _____.

110. They've been a _____ story all season.

Sports Cliché Quiz
Answers

1. way
2. counting
3. stretch
4. wire
5. panic or quit
6. excuses
7. wanted
8. fears or nightmares
9. breaks
10. mathematically
11. time
12. belongs
13. hang
14. nail
15. costs
16. happy or glad
17. our
18. monkey
19. void or hole
20. step or pick
21. shot
22. decision or pass or shot
23. rhythm or groove
24. game
25. cardinal or mortal
26. choke
27. exclamation
28. talk
29. behind
30. proud
31. playing
32. happy or thrilled
33. letting
34. no
35. bumps
36. grasp or understanding
37. clock or time
38. drawn up
39. weapons
40. weathered
41. coming or falling
42. bang
43. duel or park
44. page
45. money
46. unfinished
47. record
48. boo
49. dagger
50. meat
51. bowl or playoff
52. defensive
53. bone
54. bite
55. knocking
56. abandon
57. yardage
58. thwart
59. committee
60. miss
61. threat
62. dry
63. defense
64. pocket or court
65. special
66. contain or stop

67. tickled
68. ends
69. handle
70. ball
71. quality
72. lid
73. officiating
74. ducks
75. insurance
76. early
77. pitch
78. message
79. rope
80. weight
81. bat or ball
82. move or push
83. kiss
84. wood
85. napping or leaning
86. bush, big or major
87. strong
88. double play
89. soft, bad, or easy
90. best friend
91. shot or fit
92. zone
93. major or championship
94. hit
95. logjam
96. starts
97. served
98. step and level
99. gate or chute
100. pace
101. cylinders
102. team
103. sync
104. tough or difficult
105. momentum
106. season
107. plays
108. dictating
109. win
110. Cinderella

Scoring

100 – 110
Cliché King – *You hit a home run.*

75 – 99
X-Factor – *You played well down the stretch.*

50 – 74
Student of the Game – *You fell short, but there's always tomorrow.*

25 – 49
Bench Warmer – *You need to look in the mirror.*

0 – 24 Choke Artist – *There's a lot of soul searching to be done.*

Sec	Row	Seat
10	JJ	191

Best Sports Cliches Ever Order Form

Name: _____

Street Address: _____

City: _____ State: _____ Zip: _____

Phone: _____ Fax: _____

Email: _____

Quantity	Item #	Description	Price	Total Price
	5001	Best Sports Cliches Ever!		

Price Chart

Quantity	Price/copy
1	$14.95
2-9	$12.95
10-99	$9.95
100+	Call

Sales Tax 6% (Michigan only)

Shipping and Handling 8% ($5.00 minimum)

TOTAL $ (U.S. Funds)

The book can also be ordered in customized editions of any length and look. Contact us for more information.

Payment Information:

❑ Check enclosed

❑ Visa   ❑ Mastercard   ❑ American Express

Account #: _____

Expiration Date: _____ / _____

Name on Card: _____

Authorized Signature: _____

Sports Cliches Press

30445 Northwestern Hwy., Ste. 350
Farmington Hills, MI 48334
800.686.7555 or 248.737.6881 • Fax 248.539.1808
email: info@BestSportsCliches.com
www.BestSportsCliches.com